What Others are Saying About
NIGERIA AND THE LEADERSHIP QUESTION

Pastor Sunday's new book is a timely prophetic manual and a clarion call for positive change in Nigeria at this crucial time in her history. In a simple but compelling way, he uses a well researched and contextualized history to highlight some of the factors that helped shape our mentalities and sensibilities as a nation of people with corrupt values. It raises the poignant question of whether what Nigeria needs is strong leadership or good followership plus strong institutions to effect the desired change. He proffers practical solutions out of the socio-political quagmire that is facing the country.

This treatise is a timely one, given the current wind of change blowing across the country and hence should be a compulsory read for every Nigerian both at home and in the diaspora. For if the recommendations in this book are imbibed and put to definitive action, I strongly believe that Nigeria can become the giant that the Creator has destined her to be. Without a fear of contradiction, in the years to come, every person of color would

1

not want to depart this planet without making a pilgrimage to the most populous black nation on earth. May God bless Nigeria!

—Revd Sam Adewumi,
Founding Director, Harvestsprings International

Wow! This book is good enough for a thesis on transforming Nigeria from a sleeping GIANT to an awakened SUPERPOWER. Leadership Complete does not do justice to the length and breadth of expositions in this thirteen-chapter book. It is a book not entirely on leadership but a book on re-orientating and re-educating Nigerians. From the introduction page to the last chapter, it is full of factual revelations that not only open the eyes of the reader but also add to his repertoire of knowledge.

The introductory chapters paint a picture of how Nigeria, through its stages of development from the colonial era to the periods of independence, civilian administration, military rule, civil war to the current fourth republic, has wobbled from one dire state of affair to another because of challenges that appear to defy solutions or because we have been treating the symptoms rather that the root cause of our problems.

Pastor Sunday Adelaja takes the reader through different political systems of the world, delineating the various systems, the advantages and disadvantages of each, as well as the factors responsible for the effectiveness or failure of such systems where they have been applied. He provides historical facts chronologically, as well as the relationship between the nations, the ruler(s) and the people. He also touches the relationship between national resources and how these have been employed for development and national building with the say so of the people who are partners in this joint venture. It is never the case of the leaders leading without the consent or the agreement of the citizens of the nations. After the history lessons, painting of the global political, resources management, Pastor Sunday turns his full attention to what has been happening in Nigeria as he sees it.

Pastor Sunday offers a fresh perspective, a shift of paradigm and mindset to the challenges faced by Nigeria as a nation. As many other writers have written, the leaders we have are the product of our values system. To this end, he proffers that Nigeria's problem is not that of leadership but that of abrogation of responsibility by the masses – all Nigerians - and a wrong value system. Change of mindset is required. Currently, the masses see and hope that leadership will change their situation but time and time again this hope has not materialized.

No strand of the country is left out of the severe criticism for the adoption of a wrong value system, which is producing the kind of leaders the country has raised from the time of independence from the colonial masters. He advocates that we look at the country's value system and orientation and revamp or revalue them. The crux of the matter, according to Pastor Sunday, is that Nigeria must now go beyond paper exercise to inculcate into the psyche of the citizens a new value system where democracy is not the sole responsibility of the elected leaders but that of the people of Nigeria. He emphasizes that democracy is not the abrogation of responsibility of the citizen to the leaders but accepting the responsibilities and making the leader(s) accountable. "Nigerians and Africans should accept and take responsibility for the growth and development of the nation (and continent), take responsibility for their economy, advancement, and citizenry. The Leaders are charged with the provision of vision and leading direction the people are to go." He argues that building formidable and strong institutions is the way forward. "Strong institutions are the bedrock of" of effective society. A system that is abhorrent / oppose corruption is the key for Nigeria.

For good measure and as would be expected, Pastor Sunday includes the God factor – in every chapter he uses the Scripture to buttress his point. One commandment of God that filters through this beautifully written book is the need to love your neighbor as yourself and for Nigerians to express their wishes rather than allowing things to be done to or for them. There is a demand for every Nigerian to have respect for life, respect for the law of the nation and obedience to the law of God.

This is a book that I enjoyed reading and would certainly recommend to all Nigerians and for that matter Africans to read in order to come out of the "third world" classification, to come off the list of poor nation – particularly for a nation endowed with resources and wealth untold.

This should be on the reading list of colleges and universities.

—'Bola Adebola MSc.
Chief Exec Elderly Health & Social Care in the Community
Former South East Sheffield, England Primary Care Trust
(NHS) Chairman

I finally settled into my seat for the last leg of my flight to Lagos, Nigeria, for the Christmas holidays, though my long frame craved for legroom. As I started to relax after the meal, I heard some guys, two rows back, talking about Nigerian politics and referring to the then coming elections. I tried to ignore them, but I just couldn't. I had to contribute my two shekels worth. So I turned into the aisle, and before you know it, we were about seven rows deep into this discussion of solving Nigeria's political and economic problems. Each one was passionately sharing what he would do if he were elected leader of the country. Of course, that was the direction we took since we all believed our problem was one of leadership.

How I wish I had read this book before that trip! We all had misjudged Nigeria's problem. Pastor Sunday, in this book, takes the reader on a bird's eye view journey of our political history from pre-colonial days through the democracy and military rule; and with careful research laced with examples, he captured the problems we face as a nation with a surgeon's precision. Not only was I surprised to read what our real problems were, but Pastor Sunday also gives well thought out insights into solutions and strategies that will move us forward into international relevance.

Every progressive Nigerian who cares about seeing our beloved country move past corruption to becoming a first world nation should read this book. I strongly believe it ought to be a part of the national education curriculum in our schools. We all should take responsibility for our country's success. Reading this book, I believe this is a right step in the right direction. Thanks, Pastor Sunday, for the fresh and powerful insights. I can no longer pass the buck; righting Nigeria starts with me.

—Femi Akinola, CPA (Certified Public Accountant)
Owner, Harvest Time Enterprises, Los Angeles CA – a Tax and Accounting Services Corporation

It took leadership to lead Nigeria into freedom from her colonial masters. Since then, the leadership of the nation has not risen above the qualms of the former colonial masters. What Pastor Sunday Adelaja has done in this book is to diagnose Nigeria and proffer a true answer to many questions that leadership has not been able to address.

This book should awaken the true giant in both leaders and followers in Nigeria. The book is detailed but concise. It will help instill a greater sense of responsibility in not just the leaders of our nation but also the followers who would in turn lead. Awesome job!

—**Abraham Great**
President / Founder Gr8terworks Charity, UK &
C.E.O – History Makers Club

As usual, Pastor Sunday again has brought another ray of light to help illuminate the gross darkness in which our great country Nigeria has been groping since independence. Oliver Wendell Holmes once said, "The biggest tragedy in America is not the waste of natural resources though this is tragic. The biggest tragedy is the waste of human resources." This book has not only brought this quote into perspective as it relates to Nigeria but goes further to enumerate the systemic nature of its entrenchment as well as the process of mitigating the phenomenon. This is more of a manual on national development than a literature for mere information. I believe it is a manual not just for the nation, but for communities, organizations, families, and individuals.

—**Mike Adebiyi**
President, Consortium for Africa Development (CAD)

You are holding a book from a man who really knows he was sent to transform this world. He has been actively doing this in Ukraine and has caught the attention of several international media organizations, including the CNN and the BBC. If the parliaments of the Western nations that we regard as developed think Pastor Sunday Adelaja has value to add to their wisdom, I think all of us Nigerians owe it to ourselves to pay attention to what he has to say to the Nigerian populace. His active engagement as a mentor to Western government leaders, together with his accomplishments and wealth of experience, demands that the Nigerian populace give ears to what he has to say about Nigeria and the Leadership Question.

Personally, I am always amazed at the level of wisdom Pastor Sunday exhibits in his writings. From the opening chapters of this book, on a fly past the brief history on the birthing of the giant of Africa, to the last chapter on exalting the nation, you will be gripped with the simplicity of writing and the substance of wisdom displayed. Here is laid out for us all an unquestionable explanation for why Nigeria (and I dare say Africa as a whole) is where it is, after over 55 years of independence. The myth of good political leadership as a means of national emancipation is debunked in the book. With great wisdom, Pastor Sunday clearly lays out the root cause of our multifaceted issues - the cultural values that drive our national consciousness. With clear simplicity, he demonstrates the personal responsibility with which each and every one of us must participate if we are to derive the transformation we all dream about for our beloved country. A clear platform of cultivation of societal values is not only presented, but practical means of achieving it is laid out.

For the emergence of the prosperous nation we dream of, a national re-orientation of every citizen must be effected by getting the information in this book to everyone in our society - from the kindergarten to the Chief Executive.

Thank you, Pastor Sunday, for contributing so significantly to the emancipation of our beloved motherland.

—ArinzeChukwu Chianumba, PhD; CEng; MIMechE
Project Engineer, Rolls-Royce Controls & Data Services Ltd
Deputy National Director, Institute For National
Transformation, UK

In this book Nigeria and the Leadership Question, Pastor Sunday Adelaja has written another functional masterpiece. He has exposed profound hidden issues that are begging discussions which heretofore has been avoided for ages; questions that if not address will keep us in our current Mary-go-around journey since independence towards self-realization and national development. Besides doing a good job reviewing the Nigerian history the context within which any meaningful discussion must take place, he exposed some of the myths about national development that Nigerians have held on to, myths such as, waiting for a Messiah leader, the false hope that we can create a viable nation by nothing, the shear neglect of institutions and preference for strong leaders, and, mostly importantly, expecting great leaders to emerge out of poor national value system.

He asked the question: Is Nigeria ready to be a Singapore that we so admire? If so, can we endure the tough and highly disciplined environment that Lee Kuan Yew and his team created and subjected their people to that eventually made them first world nation? If such strict environment is imposed on Nigerians, would they not conspire and revolt or even eliminate the leaders?

The point is if we are ready for change we must equally be willing to pay the price. I recommend this book to every group both within the public and private sectors that seriously want to engage constructively in the Nigerian development discourse. It is full of thought provoking suggestions, ideas, and even road map for lasting change in Nigeria and other African nations. Bravo Pastor Sunday!

—**Professor Vincent C. Anigbogu**
Director General
Institute for National Transformation International

Let me start by commending you once again for a timely intervention in the discourse on Nigeria's national and leadership question through your book, Nigeria and the Leadership Question. At a time when the nation has failed to reach its full potential and bedevilled by socio-economic challenges leading to the blame game between the ruling class and the citizens, your book provides a brilliant perspective.

While it may be debatable that Nigeria's failure as a nation should not be entirely blamed on its past leaders, the book's perspective on the responsibility of the Nigerian citizen is quite revealing and worth looking at.

Nigeria and the Leadership Question is an informative and insightful work that attempts to answer the lingering question on whether Nigeria's socio-economic challenges and inability to reach her full potential is as result of poor leadership or lack of good followership. The book builds a case by tracing Nigeria's historical trajectory up until self-rule and the following years of military interregnum and relative stability of our democratic rule. The period presented the shades of leadership by the local, ethnic authorities like the traditional rulers, subsequently the colonial masters, the nationalists, military rulers and elected officials. We could see various roles played by leaders of the periods, local or foreign, and how it affected the development of the country. The followership equally played a part in the emergence of the leaders either through their dealings with the colonial masters, their support of the nationalists and docility in the face of dictatorship by the military or civilian rulers.

I would love to review the book based on the following

DESCRIPTION

You used a lot word-pictures of scenes and events by giving specific details in the chapters to appeal to the reader's imagination. I particularly learnt a lot from the reference to great leaders who failed because of the conspiracy and betrayal of their people and the information on the existence of major kingdoms before the arrival of the colonial masters. I am sure contemporary readers who may not be abreast of Nigeria's history, will realize, through as many details and background as possible, the way things were, in the events being described

NARRATION

The narration was in simple and in understandable language. Again you told stories of series of events in Nigeria's evolution and reference to other works on our history chronologically, giving the reader a sense of how it all started.

EXPOSITION

There was also good use of explanation and analysis to present your perspective on the fact that leadership was not only our problem but also a failure of followership. You presented the facts on your perspective as clearly and impartially as possible.

In fact you exposed the reader, through logic, that everyone has a role to play and issues of nation-building should not be left to the leaders alone but should be a collective responsibility.

ARGUMENT

You used the techniques of persuasion to establish the truth of your perspective and to convince the reader of the falsity of the long-established view that Nigeria's only problem was leadership. Your purpose was to persuade the reader to believe that the Nigerian citizen had a role to play in the leadership of the country and you implored them not to only hope and pray that things will improve but to also take action by being vigilant and using their vote wisely. You drove home the place of the people, the citizen, by drawing attention to the famous definition of democracy, by Abraham Lincoln 'Government of the people, by the people and for the people'. Before now l never really saw the definition from this point until you clarified it.

In all, the book provides a fresh and valid perspective to the leadership question in Nigeria. As l said earlier, it is timely given the crisis of leadership and citizenship that continues to plague the country. I believe it will make a good contribution to our quest for value re-orientation and patriotism. Once again l commend you for taking time to share your thoughts on how we can all contribute to the growth of our great country.

While looking forward to meeting and catching up soon, I pray that God will bless your thoughts and our nation Nigeria.

—**Felix Achibiri**
Executive chairman/founder
DFC Holdings Limited

NIGERIA

—AND THE—

LEADERSHIP

QUESTION

Proffering Solutions to Nigeria's
Leadership Problem

THE
CORNERSTONE
PUBLISHING

SUNDAY ADELAJA

NIGERIA AND THE LEADERSHIP QUESTION
Proffering Solutions to Nigeria's Leadership Problem
By Sunday Adelaja

Published by
Cornerstone Publishing
A division of Cornerstone Creativity Group LLC
Phone: +1(516)-547-4999
info@thecornerstonepublishers.com
www.thecornerstonepublishers.com

Cover design by: Cornerstone Concept and Design
International Standard Book Number: 978-1-944652-09-8

Printed in the United States of America

DEDICATION

To the new generation of Nigerians who will no longer have to carry the shame of a nation's leadership failure. To the young Nigerians who are determined to build a new nation and see the problem of leadership failure forever put behind them.

CONTENTS

PART ONE: THE BIRTH AND BURDENS OF THE GIANT

PART TWO: REMNANT LEADERS AND MODEL CITIZENS

PART THREE: GOVERNANCE RE-EVALUATION AND VALUE RE-ORIENTATION

FOREWORD

This book is a much-needed treatise on nation building as it applies to the African giant, Nigeria. But more than that, it is a compendium providing pertinent information and clarification for anyone passionate about Africa and other parts of the world; anyone searching for lasting solutions to the quest for prosperous and just societies. Pastor Sunday Adelaja has done an excellent job in tracing the early historical origins and political development of Nigeria, which provides an excellent perspective and backdrop, giving context and understanding to the solutions he later proffers in this book. This background brings a sense of realism and connectivity between the past and the present.

Not only does this book provide a historical perspective for Nigeria, but it also provides an excellent overview of different kinds of leaders over a historical period, reaching back to Ancient Rome and Greece in a bid to show the challenges and opposition great leaders face. It is instructive to see how the challenges these leaders face shatter the myth that leadership is the key. He quite rightly shows that great leadership without responsible followership will fail to achieve the desired results we all so desperately seek. In a profound way, Pastor Sunday equates the two responsibilities as a shared and necessary compact between leaders and responsible followers.

Pastor Sunday Adelaja goes on further in quite an untypical fashion to analyze the much-touted reasons given for Nigeria's underdevelopment and in a profound manner shows why such thinking is hollow and missing the point. He does this by examining different political systems and arrives at why though democracy is the best, it nevertheless requires a responsibility especially on the part of the citizenry that is most times overlooked. He pungently makes the point that for democracy to achieve the desired results of a transformed Nigeria the political elite on the one hand and the generality of the Nigerian populace, on the other hand, must confront the responsibility to deliberately and constructively participate in the democratic process.

When focusing on the challenge of corruption, this book makes the point that a lasting fight against a systemic plague like corruption requires not strong men, no matter how well intentioned, but the deliberate effort at building strong institutions that can systemically rout the evil of corruption.

In an unabashed manner, Pastor Sunday goes on to address the need for value re-orientation as a necessary condition for the Nigerian rebirth. Having laid the foundation for a participatory type of democracy and the need for systemic and institutionalized development, it is clear to see why value re-orientation is a key fabric in rebuilding the foundations of Nigeria.

Pastor Sunday concludes on an optimistic note - that good values produce good leaders and responsible followers who in turn, build strong institutions underpinned by the values they profess, which inevitably results in righteousness that will undoubtedly exalt Nigeria.

I strongly recommend this book to all who want to participate as leaders and followers in rebuilding our country Nigeria. Thankfully the issues addressed though primarily focused on Nigeria have equal application across the African continent and beyond.

Kemela Okara
Hon. Commissioner
Trade, Industry, and Investment
Yenagoa, Bayelsa State
Nigeria

PREFACE

When Nigeria got her independence on October 1st, 1960, Nigerians who witnessed it looked forward to building a great nation. They dreamt of a Nigeria that would make a mark in the history of our world. No doubt, many of the citizens that were born much later would have wished that they had witnessed the independence. I too have thought of the opportunity of living at the same time as the Founding Fathers of our country and how I could have contributed to our growth and development.

Today, however, I want to say big congratulations to Nigerians that are witnessing this period in the country's history. Indeed, God is a God of a second chance. That second chance is being offered to all of us today, to start afresh and build the nation of our dream.

Why do I believe that this is a second chance for Nigeria? Why do I believe that the chance we have today is not less important than the one those who witnessed the independence had? Most Nigerians would agree that the Nigerian project of the past 55 years failed mainly because of poor leadership. Everything rises and falls on leadership. However, that era of leadership failure is now surely coming to an end. I believe that the Almighty God himself has decided to have mercy on Nigeria. It is my firm conviction that with this new book on leadership in Nigeria, our country stands a better chance to forever re-address her point of failure.

If you are holding this book in your hand, I rejoice with you, especially if you are of Nigerian descent because now, you can join in the dream of the forefathers of our great nation and then contribute what you can to build the Nigeria of your dream. Leadership has to begin from and with every one of us. That is what this book is about. This generation of Nigerians is no longer going to wait for a messiah leader in politicians to come and build the country of our dream for us. No! We are going to take responsibility upon ourselves and make Nigeria great.

Another reason we should all rejoice that we are alive at this time in our history is that we are living at a time of change when the new leadership of the country is clamoring for change. That could be a testament to the fact that Nigeria is about to come out of the wilderness of leadership failure.

In this book, I have endeavored to briefly recall our history and how we have arrived at a situation where we have become known as a country of failed leadership. If we don't know our history, we cannot successfully chart for ourselves a better future. That is why in this book, you will discover that I took my time to examine all the different factors that have mitigated against our growth and progress as a nation. But most importantly, I have been able to bring to bear my experience of living outside of Nigeria for the past 30 years on the nation's situation. Having been involved in political consultations and advisory duties to many of the leading nations of our world, I think this book will show us a genuine method of resolving the Nigerian leadership problem.

I congratulate you again for getting this book, because I see a new opportunity for Nigeria to reemerge and establish herself as a nation of virtuous people. All Nigerians, especially those who are going to be privileged to read this book, have a role to play in building this new Nigeria of our dream. Our forefathers have already done a great job by laying the foundation for us. We now stand a good chance to kick start our journey to a better nation on the basis of our natural endowment. The achievements that Nigeria has already recorded in her short period of history will help us greatly in this process of our reemergence as a world leader.

I hope this book encourages you and revives your faith in the new Nigeria. We stand a better chance today to build a great nation than our forefathers did.

- Today, Nigeria is the 7th biggest country in the world by population, 1st in Africa.
- Today, Nigeria ranks 6th in agricultural output worldwide and 1st in Africa.
- Nigeria is the 21st largest economy by nominal GDP in the world and 20th by Purchasing Power Parity.
- Our economy is one of the fastest growing in the world. According to Citigroup, Nigeria will record the highest economic growth in the world between now and 2050.
- We have a great backup from Nigerians living abroad; the Nigerian diaspora has become our second biggest source of foreign exchange with over $20 billion USD yearly remittance to Nigeria.
- Nigeria is one of only two African countries among 11 Global Growth Generators countries
- Nigeria is already the number one country in Africa by the size of her GDP both by Nominal and Purchasing Power Parity.

In short, what I am trying to say is that our future is bright. In the words of Peter Eigen (Transparency International, Germany) "IF NIGERIA DOES NOT SUCCEED, WHO ELSE CAN SUCCEED?"

Again, I say that we stand a greater chance today to build a greater Nigeria than at independence. Let us not miss this opportunity.

Let's believe in a new Nigeria

Let's believe in ourselves

Let's occupy our place in the comity of nations

Let's surprise the world

Let's establish ourselves as the greatest nation for the entire black race.

Let us once and for all fix the leadership problem in our nation.

Pastor Sunday Adelaja
Kiev, Ukraine

INTRODUCTION

In contemporary times, Nigeria has been bedeviled by myriads of socio-economic and political challenges that seem to defy solutions. The scope and severity of these problems have led many, especially members of the international community, to wonder how the giant of Africa came to be in this quagmire. Some of the challenges the nation is currently grappling with include insecurity, ethno-religious and inter-tribal conflicts, poverty and unemployment, corruption and poor governance, youth restiveness, political instability, economic and financial crimes, illiteracy, environmental degradation, to mention just a few. This avalanche of challenges has threatened, and almost certainly destroyed the basic social fabrics of the country.

This dire state of affairs in the country has generated a lot of confusion, commentaries and controversies. There is no denying the existence of several literature and critical texts on the Nigerian situation; yet it seems to be all sound and fury, without a clear-cut line of action to be taken in order to address the situation. It is as a result of this that I have written this book with a fresh perspective and an overriding drive for national redemption and transformation.

The Nigerian populace can be categorised into two classes of people. There are those who talk about things as they happen and do nothing about them because they feel they are not directly affected. They marvel at the speedy decline of the socio-economic situation of the country, but prefer to merely talk about it. Then, there are those who are upset and depressed about the present condition of the nation, but are ignorant of what to do to salvage the situation. They are displeased about the status quo and wish to do something about it, but they simply don't know what to do; so they just do nothing. This book therefore serves as a rallying point, uniting the two classes of people, and pragmatically highlighting what should be done.

I firmly believe that although the challenges facing Nigeria are enormous, they certainly can be surmounted. However, this cannot be done without the collective efforts of the entire citizenry. This is because the act of nation building is more elaborate and much more complicated than the singular capability of an individual. An individual is just a single component in the structural framework of nation building. The act of nation building demands a symbiotic synergy between courageous leadership and patriotic citizenship, a synergy built upon the infallible foundations of trust, integrity, patriotism and an unyielding spirit of nationalism, with the aim of building strong social structures and institutions.

This is not the time to sit idly by the side lines and continually wish and hope that things would get better. Rather, it is the time to join the train of nation-builders prepared and determined to rescue the nation from its present excruciating fetters of corruption, poverty and underdevelopment. We must not resign to fate; for to do that is to be crippled fast. Every citizen deserves the kind of nation he gets. So, we must awaken the spirit of nationalism and patriotism, and take the destiny of this great nation in our hands in order to pave the way for its upward economic, political and social mobility.

I must also emphasise that, being a Christian myself, I believe that all greatness, whether personal or communal, must begin with God. It is my position that any nation, irrespective of its strong structures and great men, can only be truly great if and when righteousness becomes an essential substance in the components of its very existence. Unrighteousness, in all its shades and colours, will always be a clog in the wheels of progress of any nation and a perennial impediment to the achievement of its full potentials. For, as the Scripture says, "Righteousness exalts a nation, but sin is a reproach to any people." (Proverbs 14:34).

I firmly believe in 'Project Nigeria' and my singular objective is to see it survive and soar above its present challenges and emerge in the limelight of honour and glory. It is therefore my desire that this book will serve as a clarion call for decisive courage in the leadership, and progressive action in the citizens of the nation.

FOR THE LOVE OF GOD, CHURCH AND NATION.

Part One

THE BIRTH AND BURDENS OF THE GIANT

1

TRACING THE BIRTH OF THE GIANT

"A man who does not know where the rain began to beat him cannot say where he dried his body."
—**Chinua Achebe**

The above quote from the late literary icon provides a suitable background for the brief exploration to be made below. There are people who still hold the misleading opinion that Nigeria (and indeed Africa), has no specific history, culture or identity. Such people suggest that Africa was actually "discovered"- that Africa's history began with the coming of the Europeans to the continent. Aside from being grossly erroneous and denigrating, such opinion is also a reflection of imperial pride. Therefore, it is imperative to step back into time and unearth the almost forgotten origin of Nigeria before the coming of the Europeans.

A BRIEF HISTORY

While many historians believe that modern Nigeria dates back to 1914, when the British protectorates of Southern Nigeria and Northern Nigeria were amalgamated, the foundation of the country can be traced to as early as 1100 BC.

The West African region that is now known as Nigeria was once home to numerous ancient African civilizations. These included the Nri Kingdom, the Oyo kingdom, the Songhai Kingdom, the Fulani Empire, the Kanem-Bornu Empire, to mention a few.

The Nri Kingdom is regarded as the foundation of the Igbo culture. There is archaeological evidence that suggests that the Nri dynasty in Igbo land dates to as far back as the 9th century. It wasn't until between 1400 to 1900 AD that the Nri dynasty began to decline and several states that were under it began to spread across the face of the Igbo land, becoming very large and powerful economic states. Some of the kingdoms that emerged included the Onitsha Kingdom, the Arochukwu Kingdom, the Aboh Kingdom, and a host of others.

Islam reached Nigeria through the Northern parts of the country situated between the Niger River and Lake Chad. Although this region experienced some economic growth, it was vulnerable to attacks. As a result, it was attacked by Fulani jihadists in 1804 and eventually subdued by Usman Dan Fodio in 1808 and incorporated into the Hausa-Fulani caliphate.

The Yoruba people were the dominant group known to have existed on the west side of the Niger. They lived in communities and their main occupation was agriculture. It should be said that the region was also known for high levels of artistic achievements and sophistication, especially in terracotta and ivory sculpture and metal casting produced at Ife.

Some of the other kingdoms that had their early existence in Nigeria included the Benin Kingdom, the Borgu Kingdom, the Ibibio Kingdom, the Karnem-Bornu kingdom, the Kwararafa kingdom, the Nupe Kingdom, the Warri Kingdom, to mention a few.

COMING OF THE EUROPEANS

The Spanish and the Portuguese explorers were the first set of Europeans to begin significant direct trade with the people of modern day Nigeria. The Europeans traded within the coasts of Lagos and Calabar. This coastal trade with the Europeans would eventually mark the beginning of the Atlantic slave trade.

This, indeed, can be said to be the foundation of the warped value system and disregard for human life that have become a defining and deforming dent on our national life. The Europeans came and introduced the twin evils of inferiority complex and greed for wealth through the despicable means of slavery and slave trade. It was no surprise that the port of Calabar, which witnessed a regular trade in slaves, rose to become one of the largest slave trading ports in West Africa.

The majority of slaves were those captured during raids or wars and they were usually forced into hard manual labour of varying degrees and for various assignments, especially agriculture. Numerous slave routes were established throughout Nigeria linking areas with coastal ports to the hinterlands. According to the Encyclopaedia of African History, "It is estimated that by the 1890s, the largest slave population of the world, about 2 million people, were concentrated in the territories of the Sokoto Caliphate."

In the northern part of Nigeria, Atlantic Slave trade was abolished by Britain in 1807, and this necessitated many Europeans to begin to trade in agricultural products, such as palm, for use in European industries.

In 1900, the British government moved to consolidate its hold over the areas of what is now modern Nigeria. Consequently, on October 1 1901, Nigeria became a British colony. However, as at then, the country did not exist as a single entity. Before 1906, the entire Nigerian territory was administered as three separate units, comprising the Lagos Protectorate, the Southern Protectorate and the Northern Protectorate. In 1906, the Southern Protectorate was merged with the Lagos Protectorate and officially renamed the Colony and Protectorate of Southern Nigeria. In 1914, Southern Nigeria was joined with Northern Nigeria Protectorate to form the single colony of Nigeria.

This amalgamation of the North and South, in itself, was fraught with the egocentric motives of economic advantages and administrative convenience for the colonialists. Granted that, from a spiritual perspective, the amalgamation could be said to have some divine undercurrents, the human actors in the process had a totally parochial agenda. To begin with, it must be noted that the amalgamation was intended for the protectorates and not for the people. In other words, the colonial masters, under the leadership of Lord Frederick Lugard, were only interested in uniting the protectorates, not the people who inhabited them. This reflected in the divisive way in which the people were governed. In the words of Chief Richard Akinjide (SAN), first and second republic minister in Nigeria, once said:

"Nigeria is a very complex country. Our problems did not start yesterday. It started about 1894. Lord Lugard came here about

1894 and many people did not know that the British government did not originally employ Major Lugard. He was employed by companies; unless you know this background, you will not know the root causes of our problems. The interest of the Europeans in Africa and indeed in Nigeria was economic and it's still economic. Lugard came here for a purpose and that purpose was British interest. Between 1898 and 1914, he sent a number of dispatches to London which led to the Amalgamation of 1914. The Order-in-Council was drawn up in November 1913, signed and came into force in January 1914. In those dispatches, Lugard said a number of things which are the root causes of yesterday and today's problems. The British needed the Railway from the North to the Coast in the interest of British business. Amalgamation of the South (not of the people) became of crucial importance to British business interest."

Chief Akinjide further revealed that: "When the amalgamation took effect, the British government sealed off the South from the North. And between 1914 and 1960, that's a period of 46 years, the British allowed minimum contact between the North and South because it was not in the British interest that the North be allowed to be polluted by the educated South."

The above references to buttress what I earlier said about the beginning of the moral contamination and selfish inclinations of the colonizers that have continued to be the bane of our development as a nation till today. This foundational mentality of "Me-first" and "What's-in-it-for-me?" syndromes that have become characteristic of the average Nigerian in all spheres of life. Later the consequences of the seed of decadence that was insidiously planted in the minds of the first generation of indigenous leaders, as well as the general citizenry, will be pointed out.

THE WAVE OF NATIONALISM

After World War II, a great wave of independence agitation began to blow across the face of the African continent. In no distant time, the pressure of the waves began to be felt in Nigeria. The feeling in the air in Nigeria could rightly be described as extraordinary. Nigerians were looking forward to experiencing the joy of freedom; of total independence from the hegemony of the British Empire and the opportunity for self-rule.

> **What heightened these feelings of unrestrained excitement and positive anticipation was the belief that life after independence would be better, freer and richer. To many, Nigeria would become something close to an El Dorado with doors of limitless opportunities open to every citizen.**

Chinua Achebe in his book, *There was a Country,* captures the electrifying feeling of this period when he states that "Nigeria was enveloped by a certain assurance of an unbridled destiny, of an overwhelming excitement about life's promise, unburdened by any knowledge of Providence's intended destination."

Dr Nnamdi Azikiwe is regarded one of the fathers of African independence because of his unique political Pan-Africanist vision and his far-reaching influence on younger Africans who wanted freedom for their respective countries among whom was Kwame Nkrumah of Ghana. After his return from schooling abroad, he founded the West African Pilot, through which he passed across the message of nationalism and anti-colonialism. Its message spread quickly.

Other great political figures of the time such as Chief Obafemi Awolowo, Herbert Macaulay, Sir Ahmadu Bello, Aminu Kano and Alhaji Tafawa Balewa, galvanized the people and formed political groups in order to press home the agitation for an independent nation. It wasn't long before the wave of nationalism and the unquenchable desire for independence began spreading rapidly across the length and breadth of the country.

After World War II and towards the end of the 1950s, the nationalist movement and the demands for independence had intensified, and the growing waves were becoming unsettling. As a result, it was becoming clearer to Great Britain that it could no longer deny Nigerians the independence they desired. Therefore, the British government began making preparations to hand over Nigeria to Nigerians.

In 1953, Chief Anthony Enahoro, a western Nigerian delegate in the Federal House moved a motion for "self-rule", which proposed that the country should get its independence in 1956. Curiously, Northern parliamentarians rejected the motion and staged a walk out from the parliament. Their view was that Nigeria was not yet ready for independence. Consequently, tensions and acrimonies erupted among representatives from the different parts of the country, and the terrible treatment that was meted out to the northern parliamentarians and leaders that were in the south because of their refusal to support Enahoro's motion resulted in the infamous Kano Riots of 1953.

So, we see that discords, divisions and inter-ethnic conflicts, as well as the disastrous results, did not just begin after independence. We seem to have been demonstrating these limiting propensities for long before independence and it's high time we revisited these divisive value system and begin to assess how much we have lost in terms of lives, progress and developments (opportunity costs) to this unending trend of antagonism and conflicts. If there had been unity among the Nigerian representatives in parliament then, the country should have gained independence as early as 1956, which would have pegged us in history as the first to gain independence in Sub-Sahara Africa. Today, that honor belongs to Ghana. This discordant voices amongst our founding fathers, not only set us back in the move towards self-rule, but continues to reflect in every aspect of our national life today.

On October 1, 1960, against all odds and delays, Nigeria gained her independence to the joy and excitement of an elated country. All over the country were scenes of jubilant celebration in form of fireworks, traditional dances, ballroom dancing and the likes. The mood of the citizens was vividly captured in the following Independence Day speech delivered by Sir Abubakar Tafawa Balewa:

> "Today is Independence Day. The first of October 1960 is a date to which for two years every Nigerian has been eagerly looking forward. At last, our great day has arrived, and Nigeria is now indeed an independent sovereign nation.

> Words cannot adequately express my joy and pride at being the Nigerian citizen privileged to accept from Her Royal Highness these Constitutional Instruments, which are the symbols of Nigeria's Independence. It is a unique privilege that I shall remember forever, and it gives me strength and courage as I dedicate my life to the service of our country.

This is a wonderful day, and it is all the more wonderful because we have awaited it with increasing impatience, compelled to watch one country after another overtaking us on the road when we had so nearly reached our goal. But now we have acquired our rightful status, and I feel sure that history will show that the building of our nation proceeded at the wisest pace: it has been thorough, and Nigeria now stands well built upon firm foundations.

Today's ceremony marks the culmination of a process which began fifteen years ago and has now reached a happy and successful conclusion. It is with justifiable pride that we claim the achievement of our Independence to be unparalleled in the annals of history. Each step of our constitutional advance has been purposefully and peacefully planned with full and open consultation, not only between representatives of all the various interests in Nigeria but in harmonious cooperation with the administering power which has today relinquished its authority.

At the time when our constitutional development entered upon its final phase, the emphasis was largely upon self-government. We, the elected representatives of the people of Nigeria, concentrated on proving that we were fully capable of managing our own affairs both internally and as a nation. However, we were not to be allowed the selfish luxury of focusing our interest on our own homes. In these days of rapid communications we cannot live in isolation, apart from the rest of the world, even if we wished to do so. All too soon it has become evident that for us Independence implies a great deal more than self-government. This great country, which has now emerged without bitterness or bloodshed, finds that she must at once be ready to deal with grave international issues.

This fact has of recent months been unhappily emphasised by the startling events which have occurred in this continent. I shall not labour the point but it would be unrealistic not to draw attention first to the awe-inspiring task confronting us at the very start of our nationhood. When this day in October 1960 was chosen for our Independence it seemed that we were destined to move with quiet dignity to a place on the world stage. Recent events have changed the scene beyond recognition, so that we find ourselves today being tested to the utmost. We are called upon immediately to show that our claims to responsible government are well-founded, and having been accepted as an independent state we must at once play an active part in maintaining the peace of the world and in preserving civilisation. I promise you, we shall not fail for want of determination.

And we come to this task better equipped than many. For this, I pay tribute to the manner in which successive British Governments have gradually transferred the burden of responsibility to our shoulders. The assistance and unfailing encouragement, which we have received from each Secretary of State for the Colonies and their intense personal interest in our development has immeasurably lightened that burden.

Tracing The Birth Of The Giant

All our friends in the Colonial Office must today be proud of their handiwork and in the knowledge that they have helped to lay the foundations of a lasting friendship between our two nations. I have indeed every confidence that, based on the happy experience of a successful partnership, our future relations with the United Kingdom will be more cordial than ever, bound together, as we shall be in the Commonwealth, by a common allegiance to Her Majesty Queen Elizabeth, whom today we proudly acclaim as Queen of Nigeria and Head of the Commonwealth.

Time will not permit the individual mention of all those friends, many of them Nigerians, whose selfless labours have contributed to our Independence. Some have not lived to see the fulfilment of their hopes on them be peace, "but nevertheless they are remembered here, and the names of buildings and streets and roads and bridges throughout the country recall to our minds their achievements, some of them on a national scale. Others confined, perhaps, to a small area in one Division, are more humble but of equal value in the sum-total.

Today, we have with us representatives of those who have made Nigeria: Representatives of the Regional Governments, of former Central Governments, of the Missionary Societies, and of the Banking and Commercial enterprises, and members, both past and present, of the Public Service. We welcome you, and we rejoice that you have been able to come and share in our celebrations. We wish that it could have been possible for all of those whom you represent to be here today: Many, I know, will be disappointed to be absent, but if they are listening to me now, I say to them, "Thank you on behalf of my countrymen. Thank you for your devoted service which helped to build up Nigeria into a nation." Today we are reaping the harvest which you sowed, and the quality of the harvest is equalled only by our gratitude to you. May God bless you all.

This is an occasion when our hearts are filled with conflicting emotions: we are, indeed, proud to have achieved our independence, and proud that our efforts should have contributed to this happy event. But do not mistake our pride for arrogance. It is tempered by feelings of sincere gratitude to all who have shared in the task of developing Nigeria politically, socially and economically. We are grateful to the British officers whom we have known, first as masters, and then as leaders, and finally as partners, but always as friends. And there have been countless missionaries who have laboured unceasingly in the cause of education and to whom we owe many of our medical services. We are grateful also to those who have brought modern methods of banking and of commerce, and new industries. I wish to pay tribute to all of these people and to declare our everlasting admiration of their devotion to duty.

And, finally, I must express our gratitude to Her Royal Highness the Princess Alexandra of Kent for personally bringing to us these symbols of our freedom, and especially for delivering the gracious message from Her Majesty The Queen. And so, with the words "God save our Queen", I open a new chapter in the history of Nigeria, and of the Commonwealth, and indeed of the world."

POST-INDEPENDENCE NIGERIA

> **Sadly, however, the joy of independence was short-lived in Nigeria. Due to some faulty permutations by the former colonial masters in the political landscape, coupled with a drastic shift in the focus of the populace from nationalism to regionalism and tribalism, many Nigerians soon became disillusioned and disappointed with the idea of self-rule.**

The state of affairs obviously didn't fulfil the dream of the founding fathers and neither did it meet the expectations of many citizens of the country. This, to me, goes a long a way to show the terrible consequences of a perverted value system. Really, it never ceases to baffle me how all the principal actors in the configuration of Nigeria as an independent nation could expect to sow the seeds of falsehood and discord and reap fruits of peace and progress. This same trend of that continues to prevail in our nation till today – the trend where we individually demonstrate wrong values of dishonesty and intolerance and still expect our nation as a whole to be great. Great nations and strong institutions are never built on the faulty footing of immoral values but on the solid bedrock of good character and sound virtues.

I mentioned seeds of falsehood and discord because, starting with the colonialists, the key actors that dominated the Nigerian political landscape knew that there were deep rumblings of disorganization and discontent beneath the foundation of the new nation; yet no one did anything to sort the situation out. Everyone pretended that all was well, even while the new nation was figuratively being born into a well. And I dare ask: how much has changed till today? Has any lesson been learnt by the present generation of citizens and leaders about the destructive consequences of embracing wrong value systems and placing personal interest above national interest?

Unsurprisingly, within four years of independence, the nation had descended into the waiting cesspool of unbridled political and economic corruption, engineered by both internal conspiracy and external manipulation. Internal struggle for power, tribal and ethnic sentiments and violence helped to plunge Nigeria deeper into the cauldron of chaos.

NIGERIA: GIANT OF AFRICA?

There is little argument today that Nigeria is, in theory, still the giant of Africa. This is validated by the large amount of natural resources the country possesses, coupled with the abundant supply of human resources. Every part of Nigeria is blessed with some deposits of natural resources that are capable of stirring the envy of many nations.

Apart from petroleum, Nigeria's other natural resources include arable land, coal, natural gas, tin, iron ore, lead, zinc, and a host of others. It also has a growing population of over 170 million people, making it the 7th most populous country in the world and the most populous black nation on earth. These alone make it a force to reckon with in Africa and the World.

More so, in 2014, Nigeria overtook South Africa to become Africa's largest economy. As of 2015, Nigeria was the 21st largest economy in the world with over $500 billion of nominal GDP (Wikipedia). It is considered to be an emerging market by the World Bank and it is listed among the 'Next Eleven' economies set to become among the biggest in the world.

The implication of these is that Nigeria has exceeding potential for greatness by all standards. In fact, decades earlier, especially following the discovery oil in the country, many early economists and political pundits had foreseen the nation becoming an African economic and political superpower that would grow so great as to rival world powers like America, Britain and France.

Yet, in spite of all these lofty prospects and projections, the country has been besieged and battered, over the years, by diverse social, economic and political anomalies. And this has left many wondering: what exactly is the problem with Nigeria?

But I really think we should go beyond mere wondering and actually start taking concrete steps to remove the impediments to our collective greatness.

> **What we need individually and collectively is to critically look into our value systems as a nation. What are the character traits that mark us out as a people?**

There is no point deceiving ourselves — we know what our problems are. And if we keep doing things the same way by upholding the wrong values of self-centredness, tribalism, corruption, indiscipline and intolerance for one another that have become entrenched in our national life – our reputation as "Giant of Africa" will continue to be in theory, without any significant effect on the growth and progress of our nation.

GOLDEN TRUTHS
FROM CHAPTER 1

- Nigeria was not "discovered" by explorers or colonialists; its history actually dates to as far back as 1100 B.C.

- Nigeria was once home to numerous ancient African civilizations, including the Nri Kingdom, the Oyo kingdom, the Songhai Kingdom, the Fulani Empire and the Kanem-Bornu Empire.

- The West African areas that would eventually become Nigeria came under British rule in 1901. The Northern and Southern Protectorates were amalgamated due administrative and economic exigencies in 1914.

- Nigerians eagerly anticipated their independence from British rule. The wave of nationalism and quest for self-rule heightened after the Second World War.

- When Nigeria eventually became independent, its joy was soon truncated as the spirit of nationalism gave way to the wrong value system of tribalism, regionalism and outright corruption.

2

CONTEMPORARY NIGERIA: THINGS FALL APART

─ • ● • ●◉● • ● • ─

"Turning and turning in the widening gyre
The falcon cannot hear the falconer;
Things fall apart; the centre cannot hold..."
—W.B Yeats

When *W.B Yeats* penned the above lines of his poem, *The Second Coming*, shortly after the First World War, little did he know that he was making a predictive description of the fate of a country that would be called Nigeria. I will explain what I mean by this in justification of why I think things have continued to fall apart.

Nigeria, from its independence has been bedevilled by myriads of political, social, economic and religious problems. The scope of these problems has led many, especially members of the international community, to wonder how the giant of Africa that seemed so promising at independence came to be so beleaguered.

Actually, Nigeria's challenges are numerous and cannot be adequately discussed in a single chapter of a book. Some of these challenges include corruption, insecurity, violent crimes, ethnic and religious crises, poverty and hunger, poor leadership, confused followership, high rate of unemployment, social injustice, to mention just a few.

One of the major challenges the country is presently grappling with is political instability. For many years until 1999, the country's political climate kept undulating between military and civilian regimes.

> **Since Nigeria got her independence in 1960, it seems not to have been able to extricate itself from the unpleasant foundations of colonialism. The fact that the country began to encounter several of its now perennial challenges right after independence confirms the view of many who believe that the foundations of the country were actually faulty from the start.**

According to Adewale Ademoyega, a former Major in the Combat Arm of the Nigerian Army, and one of the trio who planned and executed the first Nigerian coup d'état on January 15, 1966, when Nigeria got her independence, it seemed as if the political arrangements in Nigeria had been fairly and equitably settled. Actually, a time-bomb had been buried deep into the foundation of the political edifice.

FOUNDATION OF CRISES

Instability in Nigeria's political system began right after independence. As I said before and as has been said by several other witnesses and analysts, including Ademoyega whom I had just quoted, the British neither made efforts to unite the different groups of people in the country nor established strategic plans on how the political system should work after independence. What they did instead was to plant a time bomb that was bound to explode within a short time. I will provide a detailed account of how this was done, as narrated by Harold Smith, a former colonial administrator in Nigeria who, out of a troubled conscience, opposed the conspiracies of the colonialists. He died in 2011, but, shortly before then, he ensured to divulge, in an interview, all he had been threatened to keep silent about. Here are a few excerpts:

"I am in my 80s now…in the past 'they' did not want me to say anything, but now I don't want to go to my grave without telling the truth about the atrocities perpetrated in Africa by the colonialists. Our agenda was to completely exploit Africa. Nigeria was my duty post. When we assessed Nigeria, this was what we found in the southern region; strength, intelligence, determination to succeed, well established history, complex but focused life style, great hope and aspirations… the East is good in business and technology, the West is good in administration and commerce, law and medicine, but it was a pity we planned our agenda to give power "at all cost" to the northerner. They seemed to be submissive and silly of a kind. Our mission was accomplished by destroying the opposition at all fronts. The West led in the fight for the Independence, and was punished for asking for freedom. They will not rule Nigeria!"

Smith further added: "The northerners were given accelerated promotions both in the military and civil service to justify their superiority over the south. Everything was to work against the south. We truncated their good plan for their future. I was very sorry for the AG [Action Group party founded by the late Chief Obafemi Awolowo]; it was a great party too much for African standard. We planned to destroy Awolowo and Azikiwe…well, the West and the East, and sowed a seed of discord among them. We tricked Azikiwe into accepting to be president having known that Balewa will be the main man with power. Awolowo has to go to jail to cripple his genius plans for a greater Nigeria.

In order to achieve their sinister objective, the colonialists had to go as far as manipulating the conduct and result of the elections that took place in 1959 to choose the government that would rule after independence. According to Smith, he was compelled to join British representatives that were putting machineries in place to "fix" the elections and ensure that a northerner became the prime minister. But then, since the Northern Peoples' Congress Party (NPC) dominated the politics of the North and Britain was aware that the NPC would be unable to rule an independent Nigeria by itself, they had to think of getting the support of a major party in the East or West.

This is why, in Smith's explanation, he was ordered to help the party of Dr Azikiwe (Zik), in the East, the NCNC. He explained that "They had to fix Zik of course, there was stuff they have got him for that could send him to prison … [they] forced him to do a deal with the North."

There is so much I could write about this, but I don't want this issue in itself to overshadow the point I'm trying to prove here. If you are desirous of knowing more about the conspiracies and cover-ups of the colonialists, it might interest you to know that investigative journalists and other concerned groups in Britain have been pressuring the British government to declassify the secret documents regarding these issues that are being kept closed for one hundred years. Even the British Broadcasting Corporation (BBC) had to ask this question a few years back: "Could it be that Britain taught Nigeria all it knows today about fixing the polls?" (See reference at the end of book).

But as I said, my main focus here is simply to trace the roots of much of the political upheaval and consequent socio-economic setbacks we are experiencing today with the goal of emphasising one crucial message: If we continue, as we have been doing over the years, to keep building on the wrong value system of fraud, dishonesty and corruption that was laid for us by the colonialists, we will never be able to take Nigeria out of the mire of underdevelopment in which it is currently submerged.

Immediately after Nigeria's independence, as a result of the crafty and destructive machinations of the colonial rulers, the different regional blocks began jostling for political positions and saw it as their respective rights. This led to a power struggle among the ethnic groups.

Consequently, within six years of independence, the Nigerian polity had become a cauldron of chaos, triggered by misrule, political manipulations and corruption.

The election of December 1964 turned out to be a charade. It was completely boycotted in many parts of the country to the effect that the election results were nationally unacceptable. The electoral crisis that followed marked the watershed in the nation's political history. The political and electoral manipulation in the old Western Region escalated to other parts of Nigeria and led to a national crisis, which eventually became part of the problems that culminated in the first military coup in 1966, which terminated the First Republic and later led to the Nigerian Civil War.

> **It was really not surprising that the first two tragedies to hit the political landscape of the country were a military coup in 1966 and a civil war in 1967. The root causes of both, of course, were corruption and ethnicity-fuelled agitations.**

First, in January of 1966, a group of army officers, consisting mostly of aggrieved easterners, overthrew the central and regional governments, killed the prime minister, took control of the government, and got rid of the federal system of government to replace it with a central government with many from the eastern part of the country as advisors. This triggered riots and many easterners were killed in the process.

In July of the same year, a group of northern army officers revolted against the government, killed the then military Head of State, General Johnson Aguiyi-Ironsi, together with Lt. Col. Adekunle Fajuyi, the then governor of the Western Region who was hosting Aguiyi-Ironsi in Ibadan. Thereafter, they appointed the army chief of staff, General Yakubu Gowon, as the head of the new military government.

In 1967, Gowon moved to split the existing four regions of the country into 12 states. However, the military governor of the Eastern Region (Colonel Chukwuemeka Odumegwu Ojukwu) refused to accept the division of the Eastern Region, and declared the Eastern Region an independent republic called Biafra. This led to a civil war between Biafra and the remainder of Nigeria. The war started in June 1967, and continued until the Biafran agitators surrendered on January 15, 1970 after over one million people had died.

Contemporary Nigeria: Things Fall Apart

Even after the war, simmering tensions and outright upheavals continued in the polity and the economy of the nation to date. Some of the reasons political instability has continued to prevail in the country include electoral malpractices, intra and inter-party conflicts, corruption, lack of concrete political ideology, ethnic and religious intolerance, political ignorance and illiteracy.

Actually, more than any other factor, corruption is regarded as the most entrenched and endemic of Nigeria's current challenges. According to Transparency International, corruption is the "abuse of entrusted power for private gain." Classifying corruption into three: petty, grand and political, Transparency International goes on to give the following definitions, which sadly describe the various ramifications of corruption that continue to make our nation a laughingstock, rather than the cynosure for other nation.

Grand corruption consists of acts committed at a high level of government that distort policies or the central functioning of the state, enabling leaders to benefit at the expense of the public good. Petty corruption refers to everyday abuse of entrusted power by low- and mid-level public officials in their interactions with ordinary citizens, who often are trying to access basic goods or services in places like hospitals, schools, police departments and other agencies. Political corruption is a manipulation of policies, institutions and rules of procedure in the allocation of resources and financing by political decision-makers, who abuse their position to sustain their power, status and wealth.

Again, let me ask: Is there any of these forms of corruption that is not found in our individual and collective way of life as a people? And do we still pretend not to know why the country seems chronically sick? Corruption is one problem that has eaten extremely deep into the fabrics of Nigeria, and the resultant effect has been devastating, reverberating all over the nooks and cranny of the country. Transparency International placed Nigeria 136th out of 175 countries ranked in the 2014 Corruption Perception Index (CPI).

Since the period of colonialism, corruption has become an institutionalised contagion in every segment of the Nigerian society. From the federal to the local governments; from the public to the private sectors; from educational to religious organisations, corruption has become the order of the day; it has permeated even the most remote rural communities in Nigeria.

A short while ago, a former governor of Nigeria's central bank, Sanusi Lamido Sanusi, alleged that billions of dollars, which were supposed to be remitted to the Federation Account, were not remitted. He emphatically stated that the money could actually not be accounted for. Up until the time of writing this book, the money is yet to be accounted for.

Many public officials in public institutions, such as the police and the immigration service, now demand for bribes before engaging in their legitimate duties. Yet these are supposed to be the people to enforce law and order in the nation. The fact that many of the shameful acts of corruption are committed in public glare without any form of shame or restriction speaks volume of its acceptance by the society.

More disheartening is the situation whereby some parents use unorthodox means to support and influence their children's performance in examinations such as WAEC, NECO and JAMB. Many purposely enrol their children in costly 'special centres', which guarantee success by aiding and abetting malpractices in these examinations in connivance with officials of these examination bodies.

Even within the university community, where character and integrity should ordinarily have been a given, corruption has been given a conducive place to fester and reproduce. Students use different methods to "buy marks" in order to increase their grades and there are lecturers who do not see anything wrong in this. In fact, some lecturers directly and indirectly demand that students pay, either in kind or in cash, before they can pass their courses.

Other manifestations of corruption include inflation of costs of government contracts, frauds and falsification of accounts in the public service, taking of bribes and perversion of justice among the organs for administering justice, over-invoicing of goods, foreign exchange swindling, and smuggling in business and industrial sectors etc.

The Nigerian ruling class is part of the reason corruption has continued to grow unabated. Political scholar and author, Oyinlola Ayobami, was quite correct when he stated that the Nigerian "ruling elite lack the kind of philosophical and ideological vision and orientation that is committed to developing "a dream society." They have no dream beyond the satisfaction of desires".

Some other reasons corruption has continued to fester in Nigeria include but not limited to the following: insincerity of government, weak government institutions, lack of transparency in the public service, ineffective and cumbersome political processes, acceptance of corruption by majority of the public, poverty and unemployment, nepotism ethnic and religious biases, ineffective and a lopsided justice system.

Expectedly, corruption has continued to impact the Nigerian society in so many negative ways. It has corroded its social fabric and destroyed public trust in national institutions and the political system. Ultimately, it has led to distrust and disconnect between the public and the leadership. The scarce public funds diverted for private gain by politicians starve the people of essential infrastructures needed to drive and boost the economy, and make life comfortable for the people.

On a larger scale, corruption has led to the loss of many innocent lives, who should have contributed to the development of the nation. Many lives have been cut short due to avoidable road accidents caused by bad roads, which had been budgeted for, but the money was diverted into private accounts and pockets.

Many have died as a result of being given fake pharmaceutical products and compromised food items which are churned out in various underground factories by decadent citizens.

Furthermore, it is unfortunate that despite all the wealth of the nation, poverty has become the lot of the citizens. Recently, Nigeria's economy was rebased and declared by the National Bureau of Statistics (NBS) to have a Gross Domestic Product (GDP) of over $510 billion (about N80 trillion), and as such the largest economy in Africa and the 21st largest economy in the world. However, this has not translated to better quality of life for the citizens; there hasn't been any improvement in the standard of living of the citizens.

In its 2014 report on global poverty index, the World Bank rated Nigeria as third among world's ten countries with extreme poor citizens. The report states that 7% of the 1.2 billion people living below poverty line in the world are Nigerians. What this means specifically is that Nigeria with about 170 million population falls among countries with extreme poverty, with over 70% of their populations living on $1.25 or even less per day.

Moreover, the report revealed that: "The fact is that two-thirds of the world's extreme poor are concentrated in just five countries: India, China, Nigeria, Bangladesh and the Democratic Republic of Congo (DRC). If you add another five countries: Indonesia, Pakistan, Tanzania, Ethiopia and Kenya, the total grows to 80 per cent of the world's extreme poor."

The World Bank ranked these countries based on their population and their share of the 1.2 billion extreme poor people in the world thus: India (33%), China (13%), Nigeria (7%), Bangladesh (6%), DRC (5%), Indonesia (4%), Pakistan (3%),

Tanzania (3%), Ethiopia (2%) and Kenya (1%). Indeed, while Nigeria, with its abundant resources, should be in this pitiable group should be a major concern for every citizen.

> **An in-depth study of the wealth distribution pattern in Nigeria will confirm the veracity of the reports from the World Bank and Transparency International. Less than 10% of the country's population controls over 90% of the country's wealth and resources, leaving the citizens to wallow in want, hunger and deprivation.**

The pathetic picture this paints is that of an average Nigerian family being unable to either afford three square meals a day or have access to the basic necessities of life.

Of course, with so many poor people, the eventual effect of this unfortunate situation is increase in violent crimes and insecurity across the length and breadth of the country. According to E. F. Thompson "Poor people are not only deprived of most material comfort of life but also cannot attain their maximum emotional and social development."

Suffice it to say that for such a deplorable economic condition to be associated with a country as rich as Nigeria, the sixth biggest member of the Organisation of Petroleum Exporting countries (OPEC), is not only shameful but grossly unfortunate.

THE RELIGION FACTOR

Religion and ethnicity have remained at the core of contemporary Nigerian politics. According to USAfrica Online, "The Bible and the Koran have become part of the staple of playing the divide and conquer strategy in the geopolitics of the country . . . long before Nigeria's political independence of October 1, 1960".

Really, it is quite saddening that more than four decades after the Nigerian civil war, Nigeria has still not overcome the dangerous and destructive cankerworms of religious prejudice and ethnic bigotry. Although constitutionally, Nigeria is a secular country, the current reality on ground where some states in the northern parts of the country are being governed under the conservative and strict Islamic Sharia law has called this to question. How can the constitution declare that a country is a secular state, and yet there are states within the same country where the citizens are governed by a religious law? Which then is supreme in those states, the constitution or the religious law? Where a conflict occurs between the religious law and the constitution, which takes supremacy? The implication of this is that it would breed religious intolerance because any particular religion whose laws take pre-eminence in the governance of a state will feel far superior to the other.

Furthermore, the scope of human carnage that has been perpetuated through religious and ethnic intolerance is almost unimaginable. So many people have been killed and properties worth millions of naira have been destroyed. I sometimes wonder why things have to get to this abysmal level. As it's often said, "How can someone be more Catholic than the pope?"

Neither Christianity nor Islam began in Nigeria. How then do we become even more fanatical than the first adherents of these religions?

In fact, it's even ironical that we pretend to take the issue of religion more seriously than God whom we claim to be worshipping in our religions. Or else how does one describe the senseless killings, maiming and destructions in the name of God that have become common in our country? Why don't we make efforts to show to the imperialist and supremacist Western nations who still see us as savages that we're indeed people of rational minds, having respect for the sanctity of human life as is being done in all decent societies? I think that if we must be fanatical at all, our fanaticism should be in sticking to the virtues of honesty, truthfulness, justice, courage, fairness and strict conformity to the rule of law.

In addition, insecurity in Nigeria has also reached an alarming state. It has given birth to a number of other criminal activities such as terrorism, cultism, kidnapping and armed robbery. There have been periods in Nigeria when reports of gruesome robberies across the country forced banks to shut down branches in several states. During a particularly bad week in November 2014, entire regions of the country were left with no open banks.

Cultism and armed robbery are sadly beginning to rear their heads even in our secondary and primary schools. These groups of criminals seek out their recruits from among members on the lower wrung of the society. They engage in other social vices such as assassination, drug abuse, rape, examination malpractice, impersonation, etc.

Kidnapping, a relatively new form of crime in Nigeria, is simply the act of forcefully taking someone hostage usually through the use of dangerous weapons for the purpose of ransom. This organised crime is increasingly becoming a lucrative business in Nigeria, because of the financial inducement that the process affords. Many times, the victims captured are secured in an unknown place, while the victim's relatives are required by the captors to pay huge amounts of money as ransom.

Most often, as a result of the failure of the law enforcement agencies, the relatives of such victims are compelled to part with large amount of money as ransom to secure the release of the victim because failure to do so within the specified time, the victim may be killed. The most worrisome aspect of this crime is that the perpetrators continue to be more daring with each successful atrocity. Only recently, a former presidential candidate in the country, Chief Olu Falae, became a victim of kidnapping. The horrible tales he told after his ransom was paid were indeed heart-breaking. As I write now, the situation continues to escalate. And I'm compelled to ask again: do we need to keep doing this to ourselves, like predators and prey in a jungle? Why don't we think of the wide-ranging repercussions of our actions and decisions as a people?

The unceasing onslaughts of the radical Islamic sect known as Boko Haram currently ravaging the northern part of Nigeria is another terrifying challenge facing the Nigerian state. In attacks carried out in Nigeria alone, Boko haram, whose name means "Western education is forbidden" is estimated to have killed more than 15,000 civilians between 2009 and 2015, with more than 1.5 million persons internally displaced. In April 2014, the sect abducted 276 schoolgirls from Chibok community in the northern part of the country, a case that sparked international outrage. However, it is very disheartening that more than one year after the kidnap of these girls, they are yet to either be found or recovered.

As I wrap up this chapter, I will, as a matter of necessity, return to the narration of the late Harold Smith on the colonialists and the Nigerian nation (all information on this is contained in the articles on his Tribute page. See reference section).

This time, however, I am not looking at what atrocities were committed; rather, I am looking at the underlying motive behind the atrocities and the lessons we need to learn as a nation. Here is what Mr Smith said on this and the advice he gave to us as a nation:

"It was my duty to carry out all of the above and I was loyal to my country. Nigerians should try to be loyal to their country, leaders and followers alike. Love your country. You have got the potentials to be great again and the whole world knows this. I am sorry for the above evil done to Nigeria. I can't say sorry enough…"

Indeed, as Smith has said, while what the British did was evil, their primary pursuit was the interest of their nation. It was and is still always the number one focus of the government and citizens of most developed nations of the world. Even while they claim to be helping other nations and peoples, they never forget to ensure that the collective interest of their nations is not jeopardized.

> **Really, we must learn, not in following their deceitful practices, but in learning to imbibe the virtues of love and loyalty to our nation. We must be loyal to the interests of our nation – to the things that will make us great indeed as a people.**

This is the secret behind the progress and prosperity of most developed nations. It's also important to know that whatever effort we make, whether by omission or commission, in hampering the peace, progress and prosperity of our nation as a whole, it will still come back to haunt our unborn children and us. As we lay the bed of our nation, so we shall continue to lie on it.

GOLDEN TRUTHS
FROM CHAPTER 2

- Majority of Nigeria's perennial challenges began to manifest right after independence, which confirms the view that the colonialists laid some wrong foundations.
- The first two major tragedies to befall the country were the military coup of 1966 and the civil war that began a year later.
- Corruption is regarded as the most entrenched and endemic of Nigeria's current challenges.
- In 2014, Transparency International placed Nigeria 136th out of 175 countries ranked in its Corruption Perception Index (CPI). In the same year, the World Bank rated Nigeria as third among world's ten countries with extremely poor citizens.
- Studies have shown that less than 10% of the country's population controls over 90% of the country's wealth and resources.
- Obsession with religion without true righteousness and godly value systems has been a major bane of progress and stability in Nigeria.

3

HOPE: THE ONLY OPTION FOR THE MASSES?

———— • • • ● ◉ ● • • • ————

"The trouble with most people is that they think with their hopes or fears or wishes rather than with their minds."

—Will Durant

Many Nigerians have continued to wonder where the ship of the nation is really headed. Actually, there are two classes of people living in the country. There are those who talk about things as they happen and do nothing about them because they feel it is not their problem. These are people who, whether by hook or crook, can be said to be financially comfortable and are thus confident that they can still get by no matter how bad the situation becomes. Of course, they marvel at the speedy decline of the socio-economic situation of the country; but they simply prefer to casually talk about it without thinking of what they can do to turn things around for good.

Secondly, there are those who eagerly yearn for a drastic change in the present situation of the country. These people are sad and angry at the present socio-economic realities in the nation. They are overwhelmed by the day-to-day hardship and drudgery they have to endure to survive. However, their only weakness is ignorance of what to do to salvage the situation. They complain and grumble but, most times, their frustrations are ventilated through wrong channels and directed towards the wrong set of people. In fact, sometimes, they choose to direct their frustrations against one another! And so, while they complain and agitate, their situations remain unchanged, and all they can do is hope that things get better one way or the other.

> **In all these however, there is the disturbing reality that the bulk of those driving the affairs of the country do not seem sensitive to the needs of the Nigerian masses. Nigerian politicians seem to have conspired against the welfare of the ordinary citizens of the country.**

It could be said that many of those in public offices harbour considerable contempt or disdain for the poor masses. This attitude of contempt could actually be seen in the way many of the politicians treat that which concerns the people. Kelechi Nwagbara, in his article, "The Nigeria's political Drama", cites an example of the disdain politicians have for the ordinary citizens. According to him, during the electioneering campaign of one of the Federal House of Representatives aspirants, one of his aides jokingly remarked, "Oga surprised me today o. Throughout five years I have been with him, I've never seen him heartily shake hands with ordinary people, not to talk of hug them, as he did today."

One thing is absolutely clear from the scene portrayed here - the deep-seated disregard many Nigerian public office holders have for those who voted them into power. Before the elections, politicians make numerous promises they know deep down in their hearts that they are not going to fulfil. They know the pitiable plights of the masses; their daily struggle for survival because of the harsh realities of the economy foisted on them by the ruling class. Consequently, these politicians hand out promises of change to the people. Unfortunately, these promises are simply used as baits to manipulate or deceive the people into voting for them, and when this is done, they renege on their promises because at that point they no longer need the votes of the people.

HOW LONG DO WE HOPE?

In reality, though, the exploitation of the masses by the government and the political elite did not begin today. As I've noted in the previous chapters, if we would go down memory lane, we would note that right from the colonial era, the masses have always been at the receiving end of government exploitation. Before independence, the colonialists exploited the people and denied them the right to determine the prices of their agricultural products before they were shipped abroad.

Confirming this observation, Shehu Mustapha, in his "Memo to Nigerian Masses", remarks that during the colonial era, the Nigerian masses "provided almost free labour for railway to be constructed to facilitate transport of goods and services to the sea for export." Continuing, he said, "they pay taxes on everything; from paying taxes on themselves, members of their families and on almost everything they own such as cattle, livestock, farmland

and household property. This exploitation was perfected through the collaboration of traditional rulers and middlemen in the name of indirect rule."

I don't know if you noticed something particularly disturbing in the above quotation. Just like the slave trade that thrived for several years in the country and on the continent, the exploitation of the Nigerian populace by the colonialists was brazenly carried out with full connivance of individuals within the same Nigerian society. What is the root cause of this?

Why would members of the same family, or citizens of the same nation voluntarily support and encourage foreigners to exploit their own people? The answer is simple: a corrupt value system that glorifies greed, selfishness and disloyalty.

There is this popular saying in western Nigeria that "If there's no crack in a wall, no lizard can penetrate it." I have read many great books, such as How Europe Underdeveloped Africa by Walter Rodney, and several others that have detailed the atrocities of Western nations against Africa over the years. While these accounts are largely credible and truly disturbing, one fact cannot be ignored: exploiters often capitalize on warped value systems to operate. All they need do is get a few unscrupulous individuals who will be willing to sell their own birth right, not to talk of their nation, for pecuniary gains.

Let me take you back to the counsel of former colonial administrator, Harold Smith, which I quoted in chapter one. One key thing he advocated was the virtue of national love and loyalty. Why do you think he gave such counsel? It's simply because he knew that the reason the British succeeded in their exploitative activities was absence of true love and loyalty to the nation by many of the so-called citizens. Sadly, this character defect is still so apparent among many present day Nigerians and the result is continued exploitation by both the ruling class and foreign nations and companies.

Let me cite a few examples. We have often heard of human trafficking from Nigeria to other parts of the world. We hear of girls and women in particular being forced into prostitution under dehumanizing conditions in European countries. How is this facilitated? It is fellow Nigerians who are trafficking and selling off their own people for monetary benefits.

What about companies owned by foreigners in Nigeria, which have become infamous for inhuman treatment of their staff and degradation of the environment? How are they able to carry on their nefarious practices unchecked? It's the same strategy of the colonialists. They bribe and lobby a few people who should be regulating their activities and even turn them to their publicity managers.

How about countries and companies that are exporting prohibited and substandard goods into the country? How have they been succeeding? Of course it's still through the same loophole of a decadent value system. In fact, I've heard of cases in which some Nigerians deliberately approach foreign companies and tell them to reduce the quality of their products or to dissuade them from destroying their expired products so they could be exported into the country and both parties share the illicit gains.

Again, I ask: what is responsible for this? The corrupt value systems of many citizens of the country. And if we will be true to ourselves, we will agree that it is this same corrupt tendencies that depraved politicians capitalize upon to continue to exploit the masses of the country.

As I noted in the first chapter, the national independence of October 1, 1960, brought with it a fresh wind of hope for the masses who had been languishing beneath the oppressive yokes of the colonialists. They had believed that things were going to change for the better since the country would now be in the hands of their fellow countrymen.

Unfortunately, not long after the departure of the 'colonial masters' the hopes and aspirations of the people were dashed against the brick walls of nepotism, tribal bigotry and religious fanaticism constructed by the political elite for their own selfish gains. Sadly, the exploitation of the masses continued.

We are now in the 21st century, and more than fifty-five years after independence, things haven't really changed much. Rather, they have gone worse. The chasm between the "privileged" political class and the "underprivileged" masses continues to expand. The masses remain the grass on which the ruling elite trample, in their inordinate quest to clinch or cling to power and wealth. The masses are in constant danger of intimidation, manipulation and marginalisation.

What makes the situation more dire is the fact that the masses seem not to have the support of traditional rulers, the business community and even religious leaders, majority of whom have, especially in recent times, colluded with political predators to deliberately exploit the Nigerian masses and keep them in perpetual subjugation.

It is this sad state that has made many of the Nigerian masses to stay aloof and simply hope that things will get better someday. They seem to be so incapacitated by their circumstances that many have simply resigned to fate. For them, hope seems to be the only option they have; their only reason to stay alive is the hope that things will get better someday.

THE MESSIAH COMETH?

One of the primary anchors on which the Nigerian masses have rested their hopes over the years is the emergence of a "messianic" leader. The belief is that once a good leader emerges all their sufferings would cease.

They keep hoping that one day there would arise a kind and considerate leader who will build a wonderful nation for them, where everyone would be happy and satisfied. For this hope, the ordinary man prays in his church, mosque and even in the secrecy of his home.

This hope is what drives him to keep on queuing up in all kinds of weather, in hope of casting his vote and enthroning this supposedly great and wonderful leader. As paradoxical as this might sound, this hope has even led some naive and zealous men to stage a number of coups all across Africa. In the hope that just in case from their ranks, there might arise that kind and great leader that would build their dreamed paradise for them.

The only problem with this kind of mentality is that it is now over 55 years since Nigeria and Africa have been hoping and are still hoping for a revolutionary leader that would bring our nation and continent to the Promised Land. If we are to apply the principle of critical thinking, we would see that it is either what we are praying and hoping for is wrong or something is wrong with our nation and continent.

> **One of the primary anchors on which the Nigerian masses have rested their hopes over the years is the emergence of a "messianic" leader. The belief is that once a good leader emerges all their sufferings would cease.**

Hypothetically, if this hope and prayers had been right, there should have been at least a few countries in Africa which should have gotten it right, especially since the time span we are talking about is not 5 or 10 years, but 55 years! 55 years is a lot of time. There should have arisen a lot of opportunities for at least a few African countries to produce great leaders, who would have built great and prosperous African nations.

The fact that this same problem seems to plague all the over 50 countries in Africa, is by itself not a coincidence. With no apparent evidence of remedy, could this be telling us that we are putting our hope in the wrong place? Are we sure leadership is truly our main problem? Even if one were to admit that Nigeria has suffered from bad leadership, does that in any way justify our penchant for blind hope and resignation to fate?

I must say it clearly that this kind of resignation is meaningless and useless. This kind of hope does not bring the required result.

> **A nation does not become great by the resignation and silence of its people. It doesn't become great even by the hopefulness of the people. It is preposterous to just hope that things will get better. The people must move into action.**

While it is good to have faith that things will get better, there must also be corresponding action on the part of the people. Even the Holy Scriptures says "But do you want to know, O foolish man, that faith without works is dead?" (James 2:20).

The ability to move any nation forward has always been in the hands of its masses. The Nigerian people must no longer sit aloof expecting manna from heaven. We must rise to contribute positively to the development of our nation. We must think out ways to positively impact our nation, instead of only complaining or waiting for the government to do everything. The truth is that the government alone cannot do everything.

More so, it's time the Nigerian people realise that the real power, the power to make or mar any government; the power to build or pull down any government is theirs. It is in their hands. The masses must demand transparency and equity from the political class. The truth is that those in political offices are employees employed by the Nigerian people to do the job of moving the nation forward. Therefore, the people should be the ones dictating and deciding what should be done with their collective inheritance.

A HOUSE DIVIDED AGAINST ITSELF

One big challenge the Nigerian masses have, while they depend on empty hope, is the bitter tree of disunity that is rooted deep in their hearts. The masses for too long have been divided along tribal, ethnic and religious lines. And this has further given the ruling cabals the opportunity to further exploit and marginalise them – the result of which is heightened disappointment and disillusionment. The political class have continued to use this divisive platform to continue to exploit the people while enriching their own pockets.

It is time therefore that the Nigerian people realise and believe deep down in their hearts that we are one nation. While it is obvious and true that Nigeria is constituted by people of different ethnic, tribal and religious backgrounds, we are equally one nation under God. Therefore, the Nigerian people must rise above the dividing walls of sectional allegiances. We must know that "united we stand, divided we fall."

> **The 'divide and rule' strategy of the ruling class must be destroyed and only the masses have the capacity to do this for themselves. We must collectively come together and speak with one voice, irrespective of our religious, tribal or ethnic affiliations; to demand for the change we really want.**

We must refuse to be brainwashed and manipulated any longer by those in the corridors of power whose singular occupation is to continue to exploit us and keep us in subservience.

Furthermore, since Nigeria is one and cannot be divided, Nigerians must learn to respect one another's way of life and tolerate one another for our common good and future. This way, we can collectively conquer our common enemies. This is the surest way to ensure the peace necessary for the development and upward social mobility of our dear nation. The earlier we do this the better for us, our children and the unborn generation.

THE SOLE RESPONSIBILITY LIES WITH THE POPULACE

As I pointed out before, the reasons why the ruling elite have been able to buy their way through in Nigeria is because the populace themselves don't have the right value system. That gives room for them to be bribed and be bought.

It is a common practice in Nigeria for politicians to give out bags of rice, money, etc to buy the votes of the people during elections. This is largely due to the fact that the society does not have a morals nor the ethics and values to stand against politicians who bribe to receive votes from the voters. It is therefore a common practice for people to look forward to sharing in the "national cake." They compromise their values even when they know it is wrong. This specific act is supposed to be enough to disqualify a candidate in the eyes of the people.

There should be a moral stand against distribution of gifts to voters in other to buy their votes. In first world countries, such acts are not encouraged mainly due to the fact that the populace of those societies have the value system and the moral stand to resist such advances by corrupt politicians. If anyone tries to do such in a developed society where there are equally many needy and poor people, somebody from the populace would be the first to report such politicians to the authorities, forcing the judiciary to act against those politicians to enforce the law of the land. Such politicians would be disqualified and barred from office because the values of the nation go against such practice.

For example, when President Barack Obama of America won the presidency in 2008, he had to vacate his Illinois seat at the senate. The then Governor Rod Blagojevich of Illinois had to appoint someone to replace Obama. However, the governor was secretly recorded on tape as saying that he had a "golden seat" and was not going to give it up without having monetary gain. He was soon arrested by the federal agents and was tried and found guilty of conspiracy to solicit bribes and wire fraud. He was impeached and sentenced to 14 years in prison and forever banned from holding any public office.

Have you ever heard of such a story in Nigeria? This is because of the difference in value systems. America has a value system of honesty that does not condone bribery, while bribery is an accepted practice in Nigeria. Just like in Nigeria, American politicians are not saints; many would gladly bribe the electorate to vote for them if not because of the abhorrence of such acts by the people themselves.

In Nigeria however, the citizens would rather rejoice that their "sons" are going to get a chance at the national cake. You hear them say things like "he is our son, let him chop." He would also be considered as a generous man. In fact, a leader who does not condone bribery in Nigeria is seen as wicked, stingy and tight-fisted, because he is not allowing others to "eat." That goes a long way to tell us how much work of reformation and reorientation has to be carried out on our citizenry. If a thorough work of value re-orientation does not take place in our nation, there is no amount of change in government that will bring us to the Promised Land.

Recently, a Nigerian ex-governor was imprisoned in a foreign country. Instead of his people to be sober and humble that they condoned and actually voted for a corrupt man, they rather protested on his behalf, even after all the facts against him were proven in the court of law. Some people even went to the extent of flying to England to protest in his defence in front of the court house. This shows the corrupt value system that is prevalent in Nigeria. If any of such people were to be elected into office, they would do exactly the same thing he did because of the corrupt value system.

Let me quickly refer to the example of Switzerland. They are known as a nation with the highest level of financial integrity, because of the efforts of the reformer, John Calvin, who ruled Geneva, which he called the City of God. The righteous principles and virtues which he instilled in the citizens of that city affected the whole of Switzerland in a positive manner. As a result, today, that nation is the most respected in the world regarding financial integrity and practices. This proves to us that the value system of a nation determines its greatness, especially its ability to produce great leaders.

In Nigeria today, when someone from your area is elected, there is rejoicing, because the people immediately assume that they will get some illicit gains. This is because they have imbibed the value system that they saw in their leaders who in the first place bribed their way into office. People rejoice when someone close to them is elected into office, because they believe they will all "enjoy".

The point I am emphasizing is that, while the change should indeed start from the leadership, it must go down to every citizen. There must be a massive campaign that will make our people to reject corrupt leaders and politicians that go against the values we wish to be known for. When this happens, the people will automatically produce upright leaders who will shun corruption.

The values of the populace determines the kind of leaders that they produce. The behaviour of the leaders of a nation only reflects the value system of the population. If the citizens do not tolerate corrupt behaviours in their leaders, there is no way corrupt leaders will retain their positions; they will be quickly overthrown, no matter the amount of military power they possess. Where the citizens can be bought however, then we see a situation where everything goes.

Unfortunately, the price of corruption is often hugely paid by the ordinary people of the nation. They pay the price of corruption when they cannot enjoy the basic infrastructures that the corrupt politicians refuse to provide for them. They pay the price of corruption when they cannot send their children to school. They pay the price of corruption when they cannot enjoy ordinary amenities like electricity, water supply, good medical services, etc.

Sadly enough, this corruption, even though might have started with the politicians, it is also endorsed by the populace. Hence, the population must also be responsible for stopping the progression of corruption in a nation.

GOLDEN TRUTHS
FROM CHAPTER 3

- The reason many Nigerians are still clinging to life is the hope that things will get better someday.

- One paramount thing that the masses hinge their hope upon is the emergence of a messianic leader who will change their lives and uplift their country.

- The fact that Nigerians and Africans as a whole have hoped and prayed for several decades without a change in their conditions suggests that the country and the continent require more than mere hoping and praying.

- For Nigeria to be transformed, the masses must take concrete steps in jettisoning petty allegiances, imbibing good values, and collectively fighting for a better nation.

4

IS LEADERSHIP THE MAIN PROBLEM OF NIGERIA?

"We must always remember that America is a great nation today not because of what government did for people but because of what people did for themselves and for one another."

—Richard M. Nixon

As we continue to navigate within the labyrinths of the challenges surrounding the Nigerian project, there is a certain belief in the hearts of many Nigerians at home and abroad. This somewhat popular belief seems to have been deeply implanted in the mind of the masses. The belief is that Nigeria's multifaceted problems can all be traced to bad leadership.

By the way, what is leadership? Leadership can simply be defined as the power or ability to organize, direct, and lead a group of people towards a shared or desired goal. It is also the "the office or position of the head of a political party or other body of people."

In addition, Martin M. Chemers defines leadership as a "process of social influence by which a person influences others to accomplish an objective and directs the organisation in a way that makes it more cohesive and coherent." Within the context of this book, however, leadership mainly refers to political office holders and government officials at the helm of affairs in our nation.

> **Those who hold the view that leadership is the main problem of Nigeria believe that once Nigeria is able to resolve the problem of quality and responsible leadership, every other thing will fall into place.**

The reason for this mind set is actually not farfetched. Nigeria, as a whole has admittedly, not really enjoyed quality leadership or stable political leadership since independence. The current socio-economic state of the country is a testimony to the fact that the political elite who has held the leadership scepter of the country has not risen to the challenge of contributing meaningfully to the emancipation of the country from the chains of underdevelopment and neo-colonialism.

One of those who hold the view of leadership problem in Nigeria wrote in his book, *The Trouble with Nigeria*, that "the trouble with Nigeria is simply a failure of leadership. There is nothing basically wrong with the Nigerian character. There is nothing wrong with the Nigerian land or climate or water or air or anything else."

Is Leadership the Main Problem of Nigeria?

Another wrote that:

"From our survey of political leadership and corruption in Nigeria thus far, it is evident that the problem with Nigeria is not just corruption but leadership failure. Corruption has attained an unimaginable height and is currently assuming a pandemic proportion in Nigeria through, and with the full support of the political leadership class since 1960. Obviously, as a nation, we cannot move on without looking back because a people without a history can be compared to a tree without roots. The fact is obvious that there really was never a golden age of great leadership in the history of Nigeria on the national level. The lack of competent, responsible leaders in the history of Nigeria with integrity, vision, high moral values has been the bane of the country."

What is clear from the above statements is that there are millions of Nigerians and even non-Nigerians who strongly believe that the fundamental problem with the country is its inability to produce responsible leaders with high moral and ideological capacity to turn its fortunes around for the better. Those who share this opinion believe that the sets of leaders Nigeria has had over the years are responsible for the present unfortunate predicament of the nation. What this means is that these array of leaders have simply not done enough to lift Nigeria out of the pit of political and socio-economic quagmire that the nation has been plunged into since 1960.

With this in mind, one begins to wonder to what extent this idea is actually true and why. Is it correct to say that the main problem of Nigeria is the problem of leadership? Would it be right to just assume that fixing the leadership challenge of the country will lead to the economic and social transformation of the nation? How can the leadership problem be fixed? Are there no other factors responsible for Nigeria's stunted and painful growth, factors that pose as much problem as the question of leadership?

FAILURE OF LEADERSHIP

To be sincere, I'm not totally disputing the fact that one of the reasons why Nigeria has remained in its current socio-political and economic condition is as a result of the failure of leadership in the country. The fact that more than five decades after independence, Nigeria, the most populous black nation in the world, with all its resources and human capacity, has not been able to extricate itself from the smarting webs of corruption and underdevelopment, points to an unmistakable cycle of leadership failure or misrule in the country. What this means therefore, is that those who have been saddled with the responsibility of leading the country have, to a large extent, failed to deliver on good governance and quality leadership.

Indeed, the political leaders in charge of the country from the period of independence cannot extricate themselves from blame in relation to the current travails of the political and socio-economic misfortune of the country. It can be said without any fear of contradiction that the various socio-economic maladies that are currently ravaging the country were allowed to fester and spread by the misrule and mismanagement of the economy by the political class saddled with the responsibility of directing the affairs of the country.

It is this failure of leadership that has led to the entrenchment of corruption in the blood stream of the country's national life. This much is emphasized by Michael Ogbeidi when he stated that "regrettably, since independence, a notable surviving legacy of political leadership, both civilian and military, involved in managing the affairs of the country at different times, has been the institutionalism of corruption in all agencies of the public service, which like a deadly virus, has subsequently infected the private sector." And one fundamental reason this has happened is because these sets of people do not possess the required moral principles and ideological capacities needed to move the nation forward.

Another way successive political leaders in Nigeria have failed the country is their inability to display the hallmarks of true and sincere leadership; that is, their unwillingness to show incorruptibility in their personal lives and sincerely lead by example. They have not, to a very large and verifiable extent, been able to exhibit the moral finesse and impeccable personal character expected of leaders employed to change the fortunes of a blessed country like Nigeria.

Another deplorable situation that has aided the failure of leadership in the country is the instability in the political atmosphere of the country since independence. Nigeria's chequered political history contains well-documented accounts of how the leadership of the country has alternated between military rule and civilian rule since its autonomy from Britain's hegemony. Unfortunately, it cannot be said which era has been better in terms of leading the nation aright. This is simply because most of those who have held the reins of government between these timelines have shown more allegiance to their private personal pockets and their ethnic assemblage than to the general wellbeing of the Nigerian state.

Moreover, there has been failure of leadership in this country because of the lack of discipline and intellectual training among the political class. This is not to say that good governance can only be guaranteed by the intellectual and educational attainment of the leader. However, from all indications, it appears that those who have been leaders of our national government have largely lacked a proper understanding of the purpose of governance. Consequently, they have not only been inefficient, but also profligate with their positions.

As Ochulor Chinenye, an analyst, once observed, good government is driven by wisdom. It requires uncommon virtue, intelligence, education, a great deal of experience and many other qualifications. In his words, "our leadership failures arise largely from the leaders themselves, from their intellectual incapacity, lack of discipline and political inexperience, not so much from the political institutions, not so much from the system. Once the operators of a given political system lack adequate knowledge and intellectual training, the system will not work." In other words, what this leads to in effect is cluelessness and ineffectiveness in office.

THE CITIZENS AS CULPRITS

However, on the flip side, while I have hitherto established that leadership poses an incredible challenge to the development of this nation, it cannot be said to be the only or even the most fundamental problem. This is because along with the challenge of leadership, there is also the problem of followership.

To continue to blame leadership without considering the warped value system of the citizenry – the indiscipline, lawlessness, docility and lack of patriotism of many Nigerians themselves - is akin to overlooking the main problem, and then giving a dog a bad name all because you want to hang it.

> **If leadership were to be the main and only problem of Nigeria, then after 55 years of self-rule, Nigeria and indeed Africa should have been able to produce a leader with the essential qualities to transform the nation. That this has not happened, obviously points to the fact that there is a more fundamental problem than the failure of leadership.**

As a young teenager growing up in Nigeria, there was no chance for me to think outside the box. I automatically found myself thinking, like the majority of the people in my nation, that our major problem was "leadership". Whenever we spoke about leadership, however, we were not talking about the leadership of schools or less significant government agencies. We mainly referred to politicians or top government officials at the helm of affairs in our nation. I listened to the theorem that our main problem was leadership so many times, that I never even thought it might not be true. It was automatically assumed to be true by most of the people around me.

> "When I was a child, I spoke as a child, I understood as a child, I thought as a child, but when I became a man, I put away childish things." **—1 Corinthians 13:11**

However, having lived outside Nigeria for the past 30 years, working with politicians, countries and governments, as well as being a student of national transformation, my mentality has been greatly altered. Indeed, having become a consultant and an expert in nation building, national transformation and factors of development and civilization, I now think differently.

Again, let me state that there is no doubt in my mind that leadership has its place in all human endeavors. My friend, John Maxwell, has popularized the saying "Everything rises and falls on leadership." I couldn't agree more. However, when it comes to building a nation, even though leadership is important, it won't be of overwhelming significance.

The role of leadership might be more significant if we are talking of a business, a company, or other smaller units of the society like the family, the community, associations, industries, etc. In these settings, the role of a leader is almost supreme and indispensable. But when it comes to nation building, leadership, especially leadership of a single man, is not of the significance we have attached to it.

I know my position in this book may seem unpopular. That wouldn't surprise me. In history, not too many people were willing to listen to this type of reasoning that I am presenting here. All through human history, men tend to simply take it for granted that a good leader means a good nation. A kind leader would take care of his people and a bad leader would oppress his people.

There is a justification for this manner of thinking though. Especially since in most parts of the then known world, in almost all ethnic groups, the system of government was based on monarchy. In such a case, the individual leadership of the monarch was the singular factor in determining the standard of living of the people.

So, indeed, if we in Nigeria and Africa today had been running a monarchical system of government, then that statement, "leadership is our only problem" could have been justified. In reality, however, our modern world has long become a post-monarchy world. Democratic system of government has replaced the supremacy of the monarchs in most countries of the world.

Is Leadership the Main Problem of Nigeria?

It is for this reason that the emergence of democracy has now reduced the all-important role of a "good" and exceptional leader in building a prosperous nation.

Even though leaders still have their place in building any kind of nation, yet in the modern world of the 21st century, the role that leaders play in building a nation is no more as paramount as it once used to be. Their role is limited, constrained or complemented by the value system — beliefs, practices, character, attitude, and general disposition — of the citizens. Whether the leadership of a nation succeeds or fails, whether the government at the local, state or federal level succeeds or not depends largely on the cooperation or otherwise of the citizens

If I ask you, reader, to mention the names of the leaders of all the European and American countries, you may not be able to mention beyond those of the big and influential countries of the world like America, England, France, Germany, etc. In fact, you may not be able to name more than ten leaders. The truth is that most people and countries like Nigeria asking for better leaders are not really ready for them. They mostly don't know what they are asking for.

Israel was a case study in the Bible. They had the best leader any nation could dream or think about. Their leader was so great and supreme that there was no country on earth that could produce a leader as good as He was. Yet, because Israel did not know the value of such leadership, they complained, they whined, murmured, grumbled and demanded for yet a better leader.

> But the thing displeased Samuel when they said, "Give us a king to judge us. "So Samuel prayed to the LORD. And the LORD said to Samuel, "Heed the voice of the people in all that they say to you; for they have not rejected you, but they have rejected me, that I should

not reign over them." —**1 Samuel 8:6-7**

Dear reader, I believe you observed what happened in this passage? The leader the children of Israel had and were not satisfied with was the Lord God Himself. He was ruling over them through Samuel. But the people of Israel were still not happy; they wanted to have a leader according to their own fantasy. They wanted a king; so God gave them a king. But soon afterwards, they were again dissatisfied with this king and demanded yet for another.

> **When people think that their only problem is leadership, that is a way of them saying, "It is only the leader that needs to change" - which means they don't need to change. It is only the leader that must pay the price of growth and development.**

What they mean by this is that it is only the leader that must work out means for their advancement and prosperity, while they are free to do whatever they like.

But then, let's consider this candid question: Have there been strong leaders in the world that worked the magic and succeeded in bringing the desired prosperity to their people? I must admit and say, yes indeed, the world has witnessed such; but, tell you what? In every one of those cases, it's either the leader was eventually killed, betrayed or rejected. Even those of them who are being celebrated today only became recognized after their death.

The truth is that most people, who ask for good leaders, don't really know what they are asking for. They do not understand what good leadership entails. As a matter of fact, when they get the leaders of their imaginations, they don't recognize them. In most of the cases, history tells us, the people end up rioting and protesting against the very leaders they once clamoured for. In some of the cases, the leaders don't die a natural death. The very same people who will later build their monuments often kill them.

GREAT LEADERS WITH CHEQUERED PUBLIC PERCEPTION

To prove my point, let me take you through history for a moment. A search for the greatest political leaders in human history, will give you this or a similar list:

1. Alexander The Great

He was arguably the greatest political leader the world has ever known. He built one of the largest empires in human history - stretching from Greece to Egypt to India. He was such a leader and military commander that never once suffered defeat in battle. He was personally tutored by the great philosopher, Aristotle. He achieved great success as a leader. His ultimate goal was to make his nation, the ancient Greek Kingdom of Macedon, a mighty and unconquerable empire. Yet he suffered series of revolt and mutinies within his own army.

One of such revolts took place in August 324 B.C. at a place called Opis. I'm citing this instance because of its peculiar nature and aptness to the point I'm trying to make. Alexander had, out of thoughtful consideration, made a compassionate suggestion to some of his wounded soldiers. Unfortunately they misconstrued his intention and, as they had done many times before, decided to insult and revolt against him. Here is how an ancient Greek author documented the saga:

On arriving at Opis, Alexander called together the Macedonians and declared that he was discharging from the campaign and sending back to their country those who were unfit for service because of age or wounds suffered. The presents he would give would make them an object of even greater envy at home and would encourage the other Macedonians to take part in the same dangers and hardships.

Alexander spoke these words with the clear intention of pleasing the Macedonians, but they felt Alexander now despised them and regarded them as completely unfit for service. It was not unreasonable for them to take exception to Alexander's words, and they had had many grievances throughout the expedition. There was the recurring annoyance of Alexander's Persian dress which pointed in the same direction, and the training of the barbarian 'Successors' in the Macedonian style of warfare, and the introduction of foreign cavalry into the squadrons of the Companions. They could not keep quiet any longer, but all shouted to Alexander to discharge them from service and take his father on the expedition (by this insult they meant Ammon).

You see what happened here? Rather than appreciate their strong, brilliant and kind-hearted leader, all he got were insults and rebellion. Alexander died at the age of 32 after witnessing other forms of opposition from his own people. The very people who had rejoiced at his leadership, ended up revolting against him, until he died a strange death at a very young age.

2. Napoleon Bonaparte

Napoleon was a French military leader, who rose to prominence during the French Revolution. He was Emperor of France and dominated European affairs for nearly two decades. He seized control of most of continental Europe. He is regarded as one of the greatest commanders in history. But despite all these, he still remains a controversial figure in most of history. He was hugely hated and had a lot of assassination attempts on his life before he mysteriously died at the age of 51. He was both loved and hated by the people he conquered and ruled. Here is the bitter diatribe someone wrote about him:

> Surely, Bonaparte is a thousand times more guilty than those barbarous conquerors who, ruling over barbarians, were by no means at odds with their age. Unlike them, he has chosen barbarism; he has preferred it. In the midst of enlightenment, he has sought to bring back the night. He has chosen to transform into greedy and bloodthirsty nomads a mild and polite people: his crime lies in this premeditated intention, in his obstinate effort to rob us of the heritage of all the enlightened generations who have preceded us on this earth. But why have we given him the right to conceive such project? When he first arrived here, alone, out of poverty and obscurity, and until he was twenty-four, his greedy gaze wandering over the country around him, why did we show him a country in which any religious idea was the object of irony? When he listened to what was professed in our circles, why did serious thinkers tell him that man had no other motivation than his own interest?...Because immediate usurpation was easy, he believed it could be durable, and once he became a usurper, he did all that usurpation condemns a usurper to do in our century.

3. Julius Caesar

He was a Roman General and Statesman. He played a prominent role in the rise of the Roman Empire. He extended the reign of Rome to England and invaded Britain. He, like all other great leaders, was very controversial despite his great success and power. And just like most other mighty leaders, he ended up being assassinated by his people.

One striking thing about Julius Caesar's death however is not just that he was assassinated, but the fact that his assassination was carried out in a most gruesome way by people who were supposed to be in the inner circle of his government. Even his supposed friend, Marcus Junius Brutus, was conspicuously among them. Another notable fact was that the assassination occurred a few years after he had successfully conquered Pompey and made the Roman kingdom more secure and stable.

The brutality with which he was killed was particularly disturbing. Someone who had contact with the eyewitnesses described what happened when Caesar was to have one of his "cabinet" meetings:

> "The Senate rose in respect for his position when they saw him entering. Those who were to have part in the plot stood near him. Right next to him went Tillius Cimber, whose brother had been exiled by Caesar. Under pretext of a humble request on behalf of this brother, Cimber approached and grasped the mantle of his toga, seeming to want to make a more positive move with his hands upon Caesar. Caesar wanted to get up and use his hands, but was prevented by Cimber and became exceedingly annoyed. That was the moment for the men to set to work. All quickly unsheathed their daggers and rushed at him. First Servilius Casca struck him with the point of the blade on the left shoulder

a little above the collar-bone. He had been aiming for that, but in the excitement he missed. Caesar rose to defend himself, and in the uproar Casca shouted out in Greek to his brother. The latter heard him and drove his sword into the ribs. After a moment, Cassius made a slash at his face, and Decimus Brutus pierced him in the side. While Cassius Longinus was trying to give him another blow he missed and struck Marcus Brutus on the hand. Minucius also hit out at Caesar and hit Rubrius in the thigh. They were just like men doing battle against him.

Under the mass of wounds, he fell at the foot of Pompey's statue. Everyone wanted to seem to have had some part in the murder, and there was not one of them who failed to strike his body as it lay there, until, wounded thirty-five times, he breathed his last."

Caesar died at the age of 55.

4. Abraham Lincoln

He was the 16th president of the United States of America. He is probably the most popular and loved president in America today, but this is only after he was brutally assassinated in office. Even though he had a lot of success as a leader including winning the war and signing the emancipation proclamation to release black slaves, yet he was so hated that he was killed for it at the age of 56.

The most bizarre thing about Lincoln's case is that more than a century after his death, there are those who still see him as one of the worst presidents in American history. I was reading a blog one day in which an American citizen posted this vitriolic comment:

Abraham Lincoln was one of the worst presidents in American history. He had no regard for the

NIGERIA AND THE LEADERSHIP QUESTION

Constitution, killed citizens for speaking out against the war, did not allow the southern states to recede, and led to inflation in America and the growing national debt... Lincoln was a very bad chapter. He did more wrong for the country than he did good... Lincoln did leave the country in shambles and it was because of him, namely, that the country was in shambles... Many presidents have disregarded the Constitution, but there are only a few more that have had as little respect for it as Old Abe.

This was despite all that Abraham Lincoln did, even to the point of paying with his life, in a bid to protect and preserve the American Dream. How Ironical!

5. George Washington

He was the first president of the United States of America. He was probably the most accomplished of American leaders, especially for leading his country to victory in the war against Great Britain, their colonial masters. He died at the age of 67.

Still, one thing you would observe in his history is that despite all his achievements, there are those who still think Washington did not do well enough as a leader. They claim he was deficient in decisiveness as a leader. To back up their claims, some have stated that it was this flaw in him that led to the Long Island massacre in which about 3,000 American fighters were reportedly killed. Some also complain about his losing of Fort Washington to the British.

6. Winston Chuchill

Churchill was the prime minister of England from 1940-1945 and 1951-1955. He was regarded as one of the greatest war time leaders of the 20th century, but despite all he did for his country, he still lost elections as a Conservative leader. As the British

Broadcasting Corporation once reported, "Labour's landslide in the 1945 general election remains one of the greatest shocks in British political history."

How did Winston Churchill, a seemingly impeccable national hero, fail to win? Between 1940 and 1945 he had arguably become the most popular British prime minister of all time. In May 1945 his approval rating in the opinion polls, which had never fallen below 78 per cent, stood at 83 per cent. With few exceptions, politicians and commentators confidently predicted that he would lead the Conservatives to victory at the forthcoming general election. The Conservative too saw the opportunity and decided that their campaign must be built around his personality.

Yet, unknown to him and to his party members, there were still many British citizens who were dissatisfied with his leadership principles. Consequently, he ended up leading his party to one of their greatest ever defeats. The result inevitably plunged him into depression and his party into shock.

7. Otto Von Bismarck

He was a Prussian statesman who ruled Germany and European affairs in the 19th century. He was prime minister of Prussia (1862–73, 1873–90) and founder and first chancellor (1871–90) of the German Empire. He is credited for uniting Germany, making Germany a country to reckon with in Europe and the world. The Encyclopaedia Britannica has it that:

> When Bismarck became prime minister of Prussia in 1862, the kingdom was universally considered the weakest of the five European powers. Less than nine years later, Prussia had been victorious in three wars, and a unified German Empire had emerged in the heart of Europe, arousing envy and fear among its rivals.

But as much as he did for his country he was forced to

abdicate his position and resign his position of service to his country in 1890. He died at the old age of 83.

8. Adolf Hitler

He was an Austrian-born German politician who was a chancellor of Germany from 1933 to 1945. He rebuilt the economy of Germany and built the country into a military might. In a speech he gave on April 28, 1939, he presented the following list of what he felt were his accomplishments as a leader, much of which was true:

> I overcame chaos in Germany, restored order, enormously raised production in all fields of our national economy...I succeeded in completely resettling in useful production those 7 million unemployed who so touched our hearts...I have not only politically united the German nation but also rearmed it militarily, and I have further tried to liquidate that Treaty sheet by sheet whose 448 Articles contain the vilest rape that nations and human beings have ever been expected to submit to. I have restored to the Reich the provinces grabbed from us in 1919; I have led millions of deeply unhappy Germans, who have been snatched away from us, back into the Fatherland; I have restored the thousand year old historical unity of German living space; and I have attempted to accomplish all that without shedding blood and without inflicting the sufferings of war on my people or any other. I have accomplished all this, as one who 21 years ago still an unknown worker and soldier of my people, by my own efforts.

However in the name of the greatness of Germany, Hitler led his country to a war that resulted in the death of almost 30 million people. He committed suicide in 1945 during the war. He is probably the most hated leader in the world up till now.

9. Joseph Stalin

He was a supreme ruler of the former Soviet Union. He turned the Soviet Union into a superpower. Under him, the Soviet Union became modernised and advanced with great speed. He changed the Soviet Union from an undeveloped country into one of the world's great industrial and military powers. He began collective farms and women's roles expanded. He declared men and women equal. By the end of his life, the Soviet Union had become an important industrial country in the world, second only to the United States.

Sadly, even though Stalin built a great country, he did so at the expense of the blood of millions. He launched the Great Purge, a campaign of terror directed at eliminating anyone who threatened his power. Today, his monuments are being destroyed and his name removed from history books.

10. Mao Zedong

He was a Chinese Communist revolutionary. He was the founding father of the People's Republic of China, which he governed as Chairman of the Communist Party of China from its establishment in 1949 until his death in 1976. He turned China into a great industrial country. He is credited for devising the pattern of struggle based on guerrilla warfare in the countryside that ultimately led to victory in the civil war and thereby to the overthrow of the Nationalists, the distribution of land to the peasants, and the restoration of China's independence and sovereignty. His goals of combating bureaucracy, encouraging popular participation, and stressing China's self-reliance greatly helped his country, as well as the industrialization that began during his reign which lay a foundation for China's development in the late 20th century.

Sadly, the way Mao went about his government and achievements were often violent and deadly. He is blamed for the deaths of tens of millions due to famine following his Great Leap Forward, a campaign to transform the society from a rural one to a socialist industrial one, and the decade of chaos known as the Cultural Revolution, a movement to revitalise the revolutionary values of the Communist Party in mid-1960s. Today, he is both loved and hated all over the world. He died in 1976 at the age of 82.

The history of these leaders clearly proves the very same point that I have elaborated above. When people clamour for a good leader, the good leader would either eventually become bad, hated and rejected or the same people who called for him would oust him. Even though most of these people I described are now regarded as some of the greatest political leaders of their nations and in the world, they are as controversial as they are great. In most cases, they were only recognized as great only after their death.

The bottom-line is that, in most cases when we ask for great leaders, we are actually asking for dictators. Most of the leaders mentioned above were actually dictators.

11. Lee Kuan Yew Of Singapore

The example of Lee Kuan Yew of Singapore, who built his country from third world to first world, is a modern example that you cannot have a great leader without some excesses. He was a dictator that ruled Singapore for over 30 years. Yet, as the CNN once reported of him, he is remembered as the man "who transformed a mosquito-ridden colonial trading post into a prosperous financial center with clean streets, shimmering skyscrapers and a stable government." He presided over Singapore's bitter split from Malaysia in 1965 and molded the independent country into the global economic powerhouse it is today.

Lee told the CNN in 2008: "I was trying to create, in a third-world situation, a first-world oasis." During a meeting with President Barack Obama in October 2009, Obama attested to Lee's greatness. He said, "This is one of the legendary figures of Asia in the 20th and 21st centuries. He is somebody who helped to trigger the Asian economic miracle."

Yet, in the process of accomplishing his numerous feats, Lee was known to be brutal towards the media, the opposition and anyone who was critical of his methods. Many in fact saw his death on March 23, 2015 as the passing of a ruthless tyrant. But for others, it was the powerful leader's final reward. The Guardian Newspaper of the UK said of him:

> Of all the benevolent dictators in history, none deserve the title more than Mr Lee. For 31 years, he ruled as prime minister of Singapore, and for two more decades, he held a key position in the cabinet. Firmly entrenched, and with a free hand, Lee moulded Singapore in his own image and made it what it is today – a prosperous city-state with an intensely pragmatic people under the spell of a peculiar brand of "soft" authoritarianism.

The question is, can we afford to have such a leader in Africa or Nigeria? Would he be allowed to successfully execute his progress policies and programs without being killed or ousted from power? The answer, of course, is a resounding NO. As it will be evident from the instances and illustrations I shall soon be providing, Nigerians, with our current value system that seems to celebrate corruption, tribalism and indiscipline, are really not willing to pay the price of having a visionary leader that will enshrine and enforce the principles of national transformation.

IN DEMOCRACY, BLAME PEOPLE, NOT LEADERS!

In a democracy, power resides with the people and then to their elected representatives. According to the Ex-American president, Abraham Lincoln, democracy is the "Government of the people, by the people and for the people." This definition places enormous responsibility on the people. Government should be about the people; the people should control it, and it should be about the welfare of the people.

Consequently, the people should be active in governance or in the way they are being governed. It behooves the citizens to, first of all, determine who gets to the position of leadership; thereafter, they must check the activities of those in leadership positions and call them to order when things are not going the right way. The citizens carry the responsibility to hold the leadership accountable to them. Failure to do this is the failure of the citizens and not the leaders.

From the foregoing, it is glaring that the Nigerian citizenry cannot be excused from the reason the nation has continued to totter. In fact, as I will be proving shortly, the Nigerian nation has actually had outstanding leaders who had great plans of reviving the nation's economy and campaigning for social transformation. However, due to the unwillingness of the majority of the citizens to jettison their wrong value systems and embrace the price of change, the efforts of these past leaders came to futility.

The point I am emphasizing therefore is that good governance alone does not guarantee the holistic development of a nation. There must be what I call responsible followership by the citizens. One cannot do without the other in the process of an all-inclusive development of a nation. Unfortunately, ours is a citizenry that is divided by the destructive values of selfishness, tribalism, indiscipline and corruption. We constantly have situations in our country where citizens vote individuals into power simply because of ethnic and religious sentiments and not because such individuals have the capacity and qualification to be effective in the desired position. We have seen situations where citizens see criticisms of certain errant public office holders as a calculated affront against their ethnic identities.

In Nigeria today, there remain wide chasms of distrust within the different ethnic nationalities, and very strong vestiges of tribal divisions. As I pointed out already, politicians at different times have exploited these unfortunate loopholes among the people. Yet, we still turn around to lay all the blame of the problems facing our nation at the doorstep of leadership? This, in itself, is an evidence of a wrong value system. A wrong value system that refuses to accept responsibility for personal failure but would rather pass the buck to someone else.

POWER OF THE CITIZENS

It must be emphasized once again that the failure of leadership in this country, is a failure of the citizens. Leaders are not angels. They do not drop from the skies. Leaders are a product of their environment; they emerge from among the citizens. Therefore, if the leaders are corrupt, it is because the citizens are corrupt. By the same parity of reasoning, if the leaders fail, it is because the citizens have failed as well in their civic responsibilities.

More so, for citizens to abdicate their civic responsibilities to their fatherland and simply believe that the government should be responsible for providing everything for them, including putting food on their table, is one of the repulsive symptoms of lazy and irresponsible followership. No nation ever grows to maximum capacity when its citizens have this kind of mind set. When in his inaugural address, John F. Kennedy, the 35th president of the United States of America, said "ask not what your country can do for you, ask what you can do for your country", what he was saying in essence was that citizens have a responsibility, a duty towards their country. This is patriotism; love for one's country directed by responsibility.

It is true that good and responsible citizenry can compel the leadership of any nation to do the right thing at a particular time. By the same parity of reasoning, an irresponsible and amoral citizenry will derail any government.

In the Holy Scriptures, we have the story of King Saul, the first King of Israel, who was commanded by God to "go and smite Amalek, and utterly destroy all that they have, and spare them not" (1 Samuel 15:3). However, instead of completely obeying the words of the Lord, he spared Agag, the King of Amalek "and the best of the sheep, and of the oxen, and of the fatlings, and the lambs, and all that was good, and would not utterly destroy them."

This singular act of gross disobedience kindled the anger of God, who through Prophet Samuel, scolded King Saul for such impunity. Unfortunately, in his reply, Saul blamed the people for the ugly incident. This incident eventually culminated in God's rejection of Saul from being King of Israel.

This story above clearly reveals the consequences of a failed leadership caused by irresponsible followership. Saul failed in his responsibility as a leader because the onus of leading the people, directing them towards achieving the desired result, rested squarely on his shoulders. It was he who got the directive from God. It was he who led the people to battle. It was he who was the king. The buck stopped right on his table. But instead of taking initiative, he allowed the people dictate to him. He abdicated his leadership responsibility to the people, but unfortunately for him, in this instance, the people failed him - they didn't make the right decision.

The bottom-line of all I'm saying is that while many leaders in this country have significantly failed, the citizens themselves have largely failed by not imbibing godly virtues, character and conducts expected of responsible citizens. This shows that they have not risen to the challenge of service and responsibility to the nation. These two sides of the coin are essential to the upward social mobility and the economic development of the nation. They represent the two major challenges hindering the transformation of Nigeria.

Therefore, while there is an urgent need for us to get it right at the leadership level, the challenge is much more at the level of citizenship. At the end of the day, the citizens will always get the kind of leaders they deserve. A citizenry that upholds and celebrates wrong values cannot and should not expect to get saintly and successful leaders.

GOLDEN TRUTHS
FROM CHAPTER 4

- While it is true, to some extent, that successive leaders in Nigeria have mostly been after personal interests, Nigerian citizens are more responsible for the stunted growth of the country, due to their divisiveness, docility and over-reliance on government interventions.

- Leadership is not as significant in nation building as the collective contributions of individual citizens.

- In this era of democracy, citizens have more power and influence than their leaders in running the affairs of their countries – unlike what happened in the monarchical era.

- Most people who ask for a good leader don't really know what they are asking for; as a result, they are never ready for the dictatorial style he is likely to adopt and the sweeping reforms he comes to make.

- Many good and strong leaders have emerged in history, but they ended up being castigated, rejected, ousted and even killed.

5

55 YEARS AFTER: NIGERIA STILL IN SEARCH OF A LEADER

"The world is moved not only by the mighty shoves of heroes, but also by the aggregate of the tiny pushes of each honest worker."

—Helen Keller

There's no gainsaying that, like the biblical Canaan, Nigeria ought to be "a land flowing with milk and honey" – a land where everyone has enough to enjoy and to share; a land serving as a model of development for other African nations. Unfortunately, this is not so. Fifty-five years down the road, we cannot say we have made significant progress.

As I noted previously, when Nigeria became an independent country within the Commonwealth on October 1, 1960, it was with pomp and pageantry. The mood of the nation was overwhelmingly enthusiastic. Expectations were high: better days, better opportunities were ahead for every citizen. These were the thoughts in the heart of many Nigerians. Unfortunately, the expectations of the people have not translated into reality.

> **More than five decades after its independence as a sovereign state, it appears that as Nigeria transited from one regime to another, it has only moved from one pitiable state to the other.**

FIRST REPUBLIC

The era immediately after independence in Nigeria is generally regarded as the first republic. Sir Abubakar Tafawa Balewa who was the then Prime Minister headed it. This dispensation did not yield the desired dividends the nation had expected. What the nation needed at that point was the uniting force of a charismatic political national leadership. Unfortunately, the political leadership at the time failed considerably. The era was fraught with political tensions and manoeuvrings, economic crises, moral laxity, ethnic and tribal hatred, especially between the Southern and Northern parts of the country.

An author stated that, "After colonial domination, governmental pattern of the Nigerian first republic was greatly influenced by ethnic party politics; as a result, the electoral process became characterized by ethnicism and electoral manipulations that were antithetical to democratic norms."

Widespread corruption became the mark of the first republic. Government officials looted public funds with impunity. Federal Representatives and Ministers flaunted their wealth with reckless abandon. In fact, it appeared there were no men of good character in the political leadership of the First Republic.

55 Years After: Nigeria Still in Search of a Leader

Politically, the thinking of the First Republic Nigerian leadership class was based on politics for material gain; making money and living well. Consequently, within six years, the nation had been plunged into crises. The violence and breakdown of law and order that erupted in western Nigeria and the Tiv war against the oppressive Sardauna Government compounded the challenges of the Azikiwe/Balewa administration. "It became obvious that the national leadership was nearing its collapse and that the ship of the nation was heading for the rocks."

It wasn't long before events took a drastic and sudden turn. On January 15, 1966, Major Chukwuma Kaduna Nzeogwu, through a military coup, ended the administration of Tafawa Balewa. Major General Johnson Aguiyi-Ironsi thus became the new Head of State. There were some who even celebrated the military takeover. To underscore this point, the editorial of the Daily Times newspaper of January 16, 1966 had this to say:

> "With the transfer of authority of the Federal Government to the Armed Forces, we reached a turning point in our national life. The old order has changed, yielding place to a new one... For a long time, instead of settling down to minister to people's needs, the politicians were busy performing series of seven-day wonders as if the act of government was some circus show..."

However, those who thought that military intervention would bring relief and improvement to the plights of the nation were deeply disappointed as the Aguiyi-Ironsi regime failed to meet the expectations of the people. During this regime, there was a significant breakdown in the social, ethnic, and economic relations among the different parts of the country. Unfortunately, the failure of this regime led to another military coup in July 1966, and thus began the series of military interventions that rocked Nigeria's political landscape. This was one of the occurrences that eventually culminated in the civil war in 1967.

> **The most devastating political development in Nigeria since 1960 till date remains the Nigeria civil war. It was so devastating and damaging that it left the country bloodied, broken and blistered.**

Over one million Nigerians (both from the sides of the eastern region and the Nigerian military) were estimated to have lost their lives as a result of the warfare. Also, starvation, diseases and other consequences of war came in its wake. On the whole, more than three million Igbos became refugees at the end of the war. It was not until January 1970, after so much carnage, that the Biafran resistance collapsed, the leaders surrendered and Nigeria's Federal military government, led by Yakubu Gowon, reasserted its authority over the region.

General Yakubu Gowon, as the chairman of the Supreme Military Council ruled the nation by decree. At this point, many Nigerians had feared that the military was planning to perpetuate itself in power. Gowon declared his intention to hand over power to a civilian government in 1976, but until then he would stay in power until the completion of his regime's political program. In 1972, Gowon lifted the ban on political parties and political activities in order to allow for discussions that would lead to the drafting of a new constitution. Unfortunately, Gowon abruptly ended the process because the debate that ensued during the discussion was ideologically charged.

The Gowon regime was not a popular regime because, just like other military eras, there was widespread corruption at almost every level of the nation's national life. By 1974, there were various reports of unaccountable wealth of Gowon's military governors and other public office holders. These reports became the crux of discussion in Nigerian dailies. Violence and crime threatened the very fulcrum of national security and jeopardized every effort at economic and national development. The political atmosphere deteriorated so badly that the bloodless coup of July 1975 was not totally unexpected.

> **General Murtala Ramat Muhammad succeeded Gowon as military head of state. And in a short time, he had become somewhat of a national hero.**

Perhaps he could have been the kind of leader Nigerians wanted; the kind of leader with the qualities to lift the nation out of the wilderness of socio-economic crises and political instability. Setting in motion the mechanisms to allow for a return to civilian rule, he was prepared to hand over power to a democratically elected government by October 1979. Regrettably, he was assassinated on February 13, 1976 during an unsuccessful coup. (I will be saying more about him and a few others here in the next part of the book).

After the death of Murtala Muhammad, General Olusegun Obasanjo came to power. He maintained the chain of command put in place by the previous regime and also promised to continue with the regime's program for the restoration of power to a civilian government by 1979. At this time, Nigeria adopted a constitution that provided for the separation of powers among the three tiers of government - the executive, the legislature and the judiciary. Consequently, the nation was now ready for the general elections that were to return it to civilian rule.

SECOND REPUBLIC

1979 marked the beginning of the second republic, after a period of coups, crises and military dictatorship. Various political parties contested in the national elections that were held and the National Party of Nigeria, led by Alhaji Shehu Shagari, emerged victorious in the elections. He thus became the new president of the country, taking over from the military.

The second republic had many things working in its favour: it was the first peaceful transfer of power since independence, oil prices and revenues were on the increase, possibilities were on the horizon, and the new government had behind it the support and expectations of many Nigerians. Thus, Alhaji Shehu Shagari and his party, the NPN, had the uncommon privilege and opportunity to move the nation towards national development.

Unfortunately, this was not to be, as this leadership again failed to meet the expectations of the people. Suffice it to say that the oil boom, which should have served as a good source of revenue to revamp the nation's economy, ended in mid-1981 and the recession that followed put severe strains on the second republic, which eventually led to a loss of confidence in the Shagari administration; the consequence of a weak and ineffectual government. Four years later, the republic could no longer stand.

Once again, on December 31, 1983, the military dabbled into politics, truncated the civilian government and took over power, citing allegations of widespread corruption by the Shagari-led administration as the reason for the military intervention.

Major General Muhammadu Buhari became head of the new government. The Buhari regime, in its zeal to move the nation forward, attempted to achieve two goals: to eradicate corruption to the barest minimum and to fight against indiscipline.

However, by August 1985 another coup had taken place, which saw the removal of Buhari from office and Major General Ibrahim Babangida coming to power. Following the forceful takeover by Gen. Babangida, a counter coup in December 1985 failed, giving the feeling that there were still some dissenting voices in the army.

The Babangida regime faced serious oppositions from the labour unions and university students. General Babangida initiated the Structural Adjustment Program (SAP) in order to address the economic recession at the time. Unfortunately, it didn't achieve much because despite all the efforts, the nation still witnessed series of currency devaluations and soaring rates of unemployment. It should be said that during this time there was no serious effort at fighting or combating the evil scourge of corruption. If anything, what was witnessed was the pardoning of corrupt officials convicted by the previous regime and the seeming institutionalization of corruption.

ABORTIVE THIRD REPUBLIC

In 1993, as a result of the intense opposition faced by the Babangida regime, a transition program was put in place to usher in a civilian government; but this arrangement was already designed to fail because of the military governing elite's unwillingness to give up political power. As a result, the transition timetable to democratic government was characterized by revisions, politicians were banned and unbanned, and elections were conducted into local government offices on party and non-party basis. When the presidential election was eventually held on June 12 1993, it was annulled by the military junta. A situation that led to the suspicion by many that the Northerners never wanted a Southerner to emerge as president.

> **Till today, many Nigerians believe that the leader that would have transformed the country but whom we never had was Chief M.K.O Abiola, the winner of the June 12, 1993 presidential election in Nigeria.**

Indeed the election was a much celebrated one. Abiola's administrative skills, entrepreneurial acumen, philanthropic nature, as well as his likable personality, a mixture of friendly countenance and warm mien, were a big attraction for the majority of Nigerians who voted for him en masse. The election itself was monitored and endorsed by over 3,000 election observers from various parts of Nigeria and the international community and was viewed as credible.

That election was significant to Nigeria and Nigerians in many respects. First, it was regarded as the freest and fairest election in Nigeria since independence. This was because, for the first time, Nigerians voted according to their consciences, putting national interest first before ethnic or religious affiliations. It was the fairest because it was free from rigging and electoral manipulations or intimidations. Even though M.K.O Abiola was a southern Muslim who contested against a northern Muslim, he got massive support from all over the nation. Nigerians spoke with one voice, selecting who they wanted as their leader.

Secondly, in 1993, M.K.O Abiola signified hope for the Nigerian masses. 15 years before Barak Obama of America began his 'Hope' campaign in 2008, Abiola, together with his running mate, Alhaji Babagana Kingibe, had traversed the nooks and crannies of Nigeria, preaching the message of hope. It was a message that raised the hopes of the masses - the hopes of poverty alleviation. No wonder Abiola won massive support. In fact, shortly after the election, on June 14, 1993, when the National Electoral Commission published results from fifteen states on its billboard outside its headquarters at Abuja, Abiola was leading in all the regions of the country, including Kano, the home state of his opponent, Alhaji Bashir Tofa.

Unfortunately, however, by June 16, through the manipulations of some corrupt cabals of politicians who were jittery over the inevitable victory of Abiola, the same NEC that had announced Abiola as leading in the polls, was pressured into halting the release of the final results of the election. As if that was not enough, by June 23, the Babangida government had decided to annul the results of the election in a most dubious manner. It nullified all the relevant court decisions and even went ahead to suspend NEC. Protests soon erupted throughout the country as the people saw their hopes of getting a visionary leader being dashed so cruelly.

In an awkward bid to placate an aggrieved populace, Babangida soon arranged an Interim National Government under the leadership of Chief Ernest Shonekan to oversee the affairs of the nation. But the citizens had already lost faith in the regime, and that same year, in November 1993, General Sani Abacha seized power from the Interim National government and became the Head of State. Even at that, individual activists and civil society groups within and outside the country continued to demand for the release of the June 12 election result.

The National Democratic Coalition (NADECO), in particular, was at the forefront of calling for the revalidation of the June 12, 1993 presidential election. So much was the tension and agitation that, when, on May 23, 1994, the National Constitutional Conference elections began, they were massively boycotted by Nigerians heeding NADECO's boycott call especially in the South-West.

Not even the government's clampdown on pro-democracy activists could dampen the spirits of the Nigerian people who still strongly believed that Abiola held the key to their much anticipated harbor of all-encompassing transformation. Bouyed by this, as well as his own passion for the masses, Abiola on June 11, 1994, declared himself president of the nation on the eve of the first anniversary of June 12 in an attempt to claim his presidential mandate. The federal military government took advantage of this and soon arrested him on charges of treason. He was incarcerated and remained so, until his suspicious death on July 7, 1998.

> **Many Nigerians believe that when Abiola died, it was the death of a dream; the dream of a better Nigeria. His death signified the death of hope for many Nigerians who saw him as the leader Nigeria had always desired.**

Nevertheless, it can also be said that his death equally foreshadowed the birth of a new era in the country. His death sowed the seed of democracy resurgence in Nigeria and his blood was used to water its first roots. His demise was a sacrifice; a sacrifice many Nigerians and international observers see as a watershed in the nation's political landscape.

Meanwhile, as Nigerians continued to hope for the fulfillment of their dream of having a leader after their heart taking over the helm of affairs of the nation, the Abacha regime did not offer any respite to the already upset and disturbed nation. He ruled as a military dictator, suppressing all forms of dissent and refusing to initiate any form of transition to civilian government. During his rule, corruption flourished like a tree planted by the riverside. The nation's treasury was looted with reckless abandon.

Till date, the looted funds that Abacha stashed away in foreign countries are still being recovered. There were numerous human right violations, such as the senseless killing of Ken Saro Wiwa and eight others on November 10, 1995. Of course there were repercussions for such a dictatorial regime. Nigeria was suspended from the Commonwealth; the European Union and the United States imposed sanctions and suspended aids to Nigeria.

In 1998, the sudden death of General Sani Abacha was announced, much to the relief of a bleeding and broken nation. His chief of defence staff, Major General Abdulsalami Abubakar took over the reins of leadership. He proceeded to make provisions for the return of power to civilian government and also released prisoners, especially politicians who had been arrested under the previous administration.

Following the successful conduct of the national elections in 1999, Chief Olusegun Obasanjo emerged as president of the nation under the platform of the People's Democratic Party (PDP), the party which also won the majority of seats in both the Senate and the House of Representatives. This handover to a civilian government thus ended the long, harrowing night of military dictatorship and ushering the nation into a smooth take off of the fourth republic.

FOURTH REPUBLIC

By emerging as the president of the nation, it would seem that God had gifted Olusegun Obasanjo with another opportunity to govern the nation. Being a former military head of state, and a one-time political prisoner during the Abacha regime, much was expected from him in turning the nation's social economic situation around for the better. He seemed to be aware of what was expected of him, as he recorded several significant achievements that impacted positively on the nation as a whole. I will be discussing some of these achievements in the next part.

However, his administration had to contend with a lot of challenges, ranging from corruption to indiscipline and inter-ethnic conflicts. The implication of this was that even though he had the mind to transform the nation, the people , as usual, appeared not to be ready to embrace, appreciate and preserve his remarkable feats – all of which are manifestations of a value system that needs to be overhauled.

In year 2000, religious tensions and crises erupted in the country due to the imposition of sharia law in the Muslim dominated Northern states; a situation that led to a cacophony among the National Assembly, the state governments and the President. Moreover, in 2004 the government was forced to declare a state of emergency in Plateau state, which had been submerged in the fire of violence fuelled by religious conflicts and ethnic strife. In the oil rich Niger Delta region of the country, the youths had constituted numerous militant groups resisting perceived marginalisation and agitating for the control of their resources.

The April 2007 presidential election was not deemed free and fair as it was heavily condemned by the international community for being massively rigged in favour of the ruling party. In fact, according to a writer, the election "was viewed as the worst election in the history of Nigeria, with the declared winner of the presidential election, Alhaji Umaru Yar'Adua acknowledging the flaw of the process that brought him into power." Nonetheless, the PDP's presidential candidate in the presidential election, Umar Musa Yar' Adua, succeeded Olusegun Obasanjo as the president of the country after being declared winner.

Sadly, he didn't rule for long. Just two years into his administration, President Umar Yar' Adua passed away, and the then Vice President, Goodluck Ebele Jonathan, took over as president.

For about six years (2009-2015) President Goodluck Ebele Jonathan presided over the affairs of the country. Maybe because of his humble background, or because he hails from a minority region of the country, there were high expectations when he was sworn in as president in 2011.

Realizing the high expectations, the president promised not to let the people down. He subsequently rolled out a policy package tagged the Transformation Agenda. Aimed at improving the standard of living of the citizens, the Transformation Agenda was a 5-year development plan, which was driven by a world class team of technocrats under the chairmanship of the president himself and coordinated by the National Planning Commission (NPC). His ultimate plan was to build upon the Vision 2020 campaign which was launched by his predecessor and himself (then vice-president) with the goal of repositioning the country to be among the largest economies by year 2020.

However, in spite of some reputed achievements made by the administration, several indices pointed to mismanagement and maladministration. The Goodluck Jonathan's administration could not ensure security of lives and properties of the citizens, which is the primary responsibility of government. Some states in the North were ravaged and devastated by insurgency, leading to loss of thousands of lives and rendering millions homeless. In April 2014, more than 200 girls were abducted from their school in Chibok, and up until the time of writing of this book, these young school girls are yet to be recovered from their captors.

The government also could not be said to be free of corruption, as there were numerous allegations of missing, misappropriation, and sometimes outright embezzlement of millions, if not billions, of naira, by government officials. The fight against corruption was practically non-existent or completely muffled by the powers that be. That aside, the nation continued to grapple with the problems of epileptic power supply, bad roads, dysfunctional educational and health care systems, high infant and maternal mortality rates, and a host of other fatal challenges holding the nation to ransom.

On March 28 2015, Nigerians overwhelmingly voted for Muhammadu Buhari as the next president of the country. From the result of that election, Nigerians made an unequivocal statement: that they deserved a change and that they have the power to remove any government they are not satisfied with, and thereafter, install another. Now that the former military head of state has been given a new opportunity to spearhead the transformation of the nation, the onus is on him to put the right machineries of quality leadership and national reorientation in place to be able to fulfill his mandate. Nigerians continue to believe that having been gifted with the return of Muhammadu Buhari, this time as a civilian president, and riding on the back of so much national acceptance and expectations, things will take a different turn.

According to Muhammadu Buhari himself, "Nigeria has indeed entered a new dispensation… my administration does not intend to repeat the same mistakes made by previous governments."

However, it must still be emphasized that whatever good intentions and plans the present government may have, its efforts will be sabotaged unless the citizens collectively decide to cooperate and embrace the change mandate of the new government. That change must inevitably begin with change of values. Would we be ready to discard the destructive values of indiscipline, impatience, intolerance, circumventing the law (whether in the public or private, whether on the road or in our offices) and corruption? Without the full support of the citizens, there's little a government can do to change the nation.

GOLDEN TRUTHS
FROM CHAPTER 5

- Neither civilian administration nor military incursion seems to have provided the "almighty" leader that Nigerians have been hoping for since Independence.

- A few of the past leaders made some notable efforts to transform the nation but their efforts did not yield lasting fruits, primarily because of the wrong attitudes of the citizens.

- Many Nigerians believe that the late Chief M.K.O. Abiola was the best leader the country could have had but he was denied the opportunity to govern the nation.

- Nigerians voted massively for the present President, who was once a military ruler, to express their desperation for an urgent, positive change.

Part Two

Remnant Leaders And Model Citizens

6

REMNANT LEADERS WITH TRUNCATED TENURES

"And it will be for a sign and for a witness to the Lord of hosts in the land of Egypt; for they will cry to the Lord because of the oppressors, and He will send them a Savior and a Mighty One, and He will deliver them."
—Isaiah 19:20

There is little doubt that every country desires to have a great leader. Nigeria, in particular, has continued to yearn for a leader in the mould of a messiah; a God-sent leader, like the biblical Moses, with a divinely inspired calling to lead the nation to the Promised Land of unprecedented peace, progress and prosperity.

However, as I have variously emphasized in the preceding chapters, in a democratic system like ours, it is wrong and futile to expect a leader to single-handedly bear the burdens of the transformation and progress of a nation. A leader can only succeed if he has a helpful environment; if the citizens or followers will perform their own responsibilities, especially in imbibing and demonstrating good values.

In the case of the biblical Moses, he tried all he could to lead the people to the Promised Land but the people were his albatross. Moses did not succeed in leading the people to the land of promise because of the wrong attitude and value system of the people he led.

Moses was a leader in the mould of a messiah. He was the kind of leader any nation would wish for but because he had one of the most difficult set of persons as followers, he was not able to complete his mission. In fact, the Bible described them as a "stiff-necked people" (stubborn and difficult to guide).

What this scenario underscores therefore is that the task of nation building is not the singular job of an individual.

> **That a leader is messianic or that he possesses the qualities needed for national transformation will not automatically lead to national salvation. He needs the cooperation of the citizens.**

The citizens must realize that whether a leader or a nation succeeds or fails is in their hands. Just as in the case of Israel, the truth is that countries like Nigeria asking for better and messianic leaders are not really ready for them. In fact, it might interest you to know that Nigeria has had examples of great leaders like Moses in the past. Sadly, however, their reigns and impacts were short-lived because of the wrong value systems of the majority of the citizens.

Let's get this straight. There is no point waiting for a miracle that may never happen. Any nation could be viewed as a pot from where the most active, zealous or talented representatives of this given society emerge as their leaders. If the pot therefore is corrupt, only corrupt leaders will come out of that pot. If the pot however is clean and righteous and everybody in that nation is living by righteous value systems, naturally the leaders that will be coming out of that pot will reflect the nature and the environment of the pot itself. They will be clean, they will be trustworthy and they will be righteous.

Of course, to every rule, there are always exceptions. In every given society, even if 99% of the people are corrupt, there will still be at least 1% of the people that are upright.

These kinds of people, thanks to a different upbringing or disciplined and stringent background; are different from the rest of the population. If a country is fortunate enough to have such a remnant as its leaders, naturally we think such a nation should rejoice. In actual fact though, it is often the opposite that happens. As I have said in other chapters of this book, history has taught us that most of these people are usually persecuted, overthrown, dismissed or even executed in office.

There is sometimes a departure from this trend though. That is when such a remnant leader manages to prove his or her worth to convince the people of the nation of his good intentions. In such a situation when the populace accepts such an exceptional leader, his most important duty must be to change the nature of the pot by changing the value system of the nation.

The lesson I am trying to pass across in this book and especially in this chapter is that leadership is not the biggest problem of Nigeria and Africa. Our biggest problem is a corrupt value system. Our leaders come from our societies. The leadership of any nation is only but a reflection of the prevailing value systems of that society. As it is often said, every nation deserves its leader. It is a fact of history that nations only produce the types of leaders they deserve. This is because these leaders are coming from the general populace of that country. So if a nation is corrupt, it will only produce corrupt leaders because the citizenry in general are living by corrupt value systems.

Of course there are exceptions to the rule. It is these exceptions that I will be looking at in this chapter and the next. In this chapter, I will talk about the first category of such remnant leaders. These were great leaders who were bent on holistic national transformation but were eventually rejected, removed or even executed in office by the populace. Let's look at them and the great accomplishments that were recorded under their rule.

SIR AHMADU BELLO

Sir Ahmadu Bello (June 12, 1910 – January 15, 1966) was a celebrated Nigerian politician, the first premier of the Northern Nigeria region from 1954-1966 and an astute educationist who founded the famous and the largest university in West Africa and the second in Africa, Ahmadu Bello University.

As leader of the Northern People's Congress, he dominated Nigerian politics throughout the early Nigerian Federation and the First Nigerian Republic. Sir Ahmadu Bello, the Sardauna of Sokoto was a politician of distinction, unaffected by selfish interest, dedicated to service and committed to unity and the brotherhood of the human person. Since he became the President of the NPC in 1952, up to the time of his death, in the hands of some misguided military officers, on 15th January 1966 he became a fundamentalist for unity in Nigeria in general and the North in particular.

No individual ever arose from the Nigerian political scene,

who dedicated his life to the unity of his people as the Sardauna. In the pursuit of this noble goal, the word north came to be associated as a tribal name, rather than a reference to a region and this is the case up to this day. The current reference now is " Yoruba, Igbo and Northerners" thereby giving Northerners the status of a collective tribe, which today consist of more than 200 tribes. What this means is that the Sardauna succeeded in creating a united entity out of diverse tribes and this was strengthened by the general use of the Hausa language in the region.

How was he able to achieve this remarkable legacy? How did he create a common identity for such a diverse people, who lost their individual identity for the word North? Let me answer with a few examples. There was a young secondary school graduate from what is today Plateau State who passed out with flying colors. The Sardauna came across his name when he was going through the results of college examinations as he formed the habit of doing so. He was so impressed with the results of that particular student that he ordered that he be brought to Kaduna. When those ordered to do so arrived their house, his father became apprehensive, wondering aloud what offence his son might have committed that he was to be taken to the Sardauna. As the messengers had no idea, he became more worried and pleaded that he should be allowed to accompany him.

This was granted. They arrived Kaduna in the evening and straight to the Sardauna's residence where they met him having his dinner. The Sardauna was informed of their arrival and invited them to join him for dinner. Both father and son were afraid until he the Sardauna, stood up and held the father's hand and sat him down to have dinner. The son was asked to join. The two were still not themselves.

After dinner, he told them why he wanted to see the boy. The father was relieved and more so when the Sardauna showered them with gifts. He was said to have told them that "your son has done the North proud in his examination so we are sending him for further studies abroad". The lesson here is that the Sardauna was concerned in the matters of individuals in his domain and this very much endeared him to the people. The young boy was not a Muslim, a Hausa or Fulani. He was a Christian from one of the minority tribes in Plateau. Yet his achievements were recognized by a Fulani Muslim leader which consequently made it possible for the young man to graduate from a British university with a degree in mining engineering. It was exceptional that a leader would concern himself with going through school reports after each academic year and rewarded individuals purely on merit. The Sardauna saw every one as a human being and not as Birom, Kanuri, Hausa or Higgi.

GENERAL MURTALA MOHAMMED

As evening was approaching on July 30, 1975, Murtala made his maiden speech to the nation as the Head of State and Commander-in-Chief of the Armed Forces. When he came to power, he constituted the Federal Executive Council with 25 ministerial posts, 12 of which were held by civilians even though the real power was vested in the Supreme Military

Murtala soon set up a 50-man committee to see to a new draft constitution and make plans on handing over to the civilians by October 1979. The late Justice Rotimi Williams headed the Constitution Drafting Committee (CDC).

Even though he was a military man, it won't be wrong to describe Murtala as a true democrat because he was committed to his transition-to-civil-rule program. He never reneged on his promise to return the country to civil rule unlike many of those before and after him.

In fact, many political pundits continue to credit him as laying the foundation for the democracy we enjoy today given his set out program to return the military to the barracks. Though a professional soldier himself, he was convinced that the military had no business remaining in power beyond necessary.

Although very brief (just a little over six months), Murtala's time was full of events. Upon assuming power, Murtala (permit me, that flows better than referring to him as Mohammed) made it abundantly clear that he would brook no nonsense. He was very decisive with issues, wasted no time and because of this and many more, he became the darling of millions of Nigerians. His countrymen and women were immensely happy with him and were satisfied that at long last, Nigeria now had a strong, decisive and uncompromising leader, the one with the discipline and tenacity to take them to the Promised Land. He was a leader who came to power to rescue the seemingly sinking ship of the country and entrench a new and enduring political culture among the citizenry.

Without mincing words, Murtala Muhammed was, indisputably, a true democrat and a quintessential patriot who laid a solid foundation for true democracy to blossom in a nation that had wandered for so long in the search for genuine democracy. His 'revolutionary regime' purged corruption in the military and public service. He dared 'principalities and powers' in high places all for the interest of Nigeria

1. Murtala's role in making Abuja new Federal Capital Territory

In his characteristically decisive manner, Murtala felt Lagos was too dirty, rowdy and crime-ridden to be the nation's capital. He therefore put in place plans to build a new Federal Capital Territory, to be sited in Abuja. He set up a panel, headed by Justice

Akinola Aguda to consider the possibility of a new capital. Few days before he was killed, on the 3rd of February 1976, he made an announcement that the Federal Capital would be moved to a 'federal territory of about 8,000 square kilometers in the central part of the country.'

> **Even though he was a military man, it won't be wrong to describe Murtala as a true democrat because he was committed to his transition-to-civil-rule program. He never reneged on his promise to return the country to civil rule unlike many of those before and after him.**

2. Creation of Seven New States

In his quest for rapid national development, Murtala set up a panel, headed by Justice Ayo Irikefe towards the creation of seven more states (Niger, Bauchi, Gongola, Benue, Ogun, Imo and Bendel) to the 12 existing ones on December 22, 1975. The panel came up with a report which was utilized in the formation of the new states in 1976.

3. Cancelling of 1973 census

Upon becoming Head of State, Murtala proceeded to cancel the 1973 census which was lopsided to favor the northerners, after which he adopted the 1963 figures.

4. Personal Character

Murtala was a blunt, outspoken and consummate risk taker.

A no-nonsense person, Murtala was known to be a man of honour, integrity and personal conviction; he acted his words and matched his rhetoric with action. He was never found wanting in terms of taking any firm decision in the interest of the nation.

Describing him, one historian said, "He settled swiftly to do his job of serving the best interest of Nigeria and had little time for idle jokes and play; he was businesslike in speech, gait, appearance, body language and manner. He cut the perfect picture of a 'Head of State'. This no-nonsense Kano born soldier introduced the phrase 'with immediate effect' to the Nigerian lexicon. With the magic of that phrase, government decisions left the realm of idealism and expectations to become serious pronouncement of policies...Murtala, who unfortunately lived to be only 38 years old, should rather be remembered for his foresightedness, bravery, galantry, resourcefulness, decisiveness, vigour, resillience and strength of character. Murtala never stood on the fence; with him you were never in doubts as to where he was headed; he was reliable."

Another public analyst, Dr. Peter Ifeachi, once said of him that, "Murtala Muhammed, unlike many of our leaders today, was a man of honour and a trusted statesman. He was a reliable and patriotic statesman. From the creation of seven additional states, the drafting of a new constitution and the outlining of a political agenda to hand over power to civilians in 1979, one will see a man who believed in his words and went the extra miles to actualize them. But today, such convictions and actions have become strangers to our leaders."

Sadly, despite these outstanding attributes and achievements, Murtala's administration was prematurely terminated when he was brutally assassinated on his way to work on February 13, 1976. Being a simple leader with populist ideas, Murtala had no speeding convoys or heavily armed security details and preferred to stay in the traffic with his fellow citizens. This was what some people with a perverted value system took advantage of. His vehicle was ambushed by a group of soldiers and he was shot to death. The assassination was part of the abortive coup attempt spearheaded by Lieutenant Colonel Buka Suka Dimka.

That is what happens when citizens are not orientated to imbibe godly values. One would have thought that with the courage, charisma and great track records of Murtala Muhammed, he would be a generally appreciated and celebrated leader, but he ended up dying cruelly by the hands of the same citizens whose lives he was trying to transform.

It is no secret that the Dimka coup was not executed without the influence of ordinary Nigerian citizens. A lot of Nigerians were not satisfied with the ruggedness of Murtala's government. He was so disciplined that he fired so many civil servants for as simple a reason as coming to work late. So many people who were involved in various illicit activities were either dismissed or arrested. All these were achieved within six months of government. Most citizens were afraid that sooner or later the long hand of justice would reach them.

It is therefore not surprising to see a lot of civilians, especially civil servants and politicians clamoring for his removal. Today, it is rather surprising that people will clamor for the removal of such a visionary leader. That is what happens when a leader comes on the scene whose value systems differ from the values of the ordinary people. The people will rather see what he is doing as a disturbance of their lifestyles. Yes, Murtala indeed disrupted the lifestyle of a lot of people, but what was the reason behind it? It was to provide a better standard of living for the generality of Nigerians. That never happened for the simple reason that those whose lifestyles were geared towards thinking only of themselves, rather than thinking of the gain of the general populace, would not let him be.

As good as a remnant leader is, this is one of the sad scenarios of their end when the value system of the general populace remains unchanged. There are other scenarios that we will see as we move on in this book.

The next government I will be talking about is the government of Buhari/Idiagbon (1983-1985).

GENERAL MUHAMMADU BUHARI

It was not such a huge surprise that Muhammadu Buhari in early 2015 became the first presidential candidate to defeat an incumbent president in an election that was generally hailed as free and fair. Many Nigerians still continue to have nostalgic feelings about his tenure as military head of state in the mid-80s. It was the golden era of discipline, responsibility and accountability in every sector and circle in the country; a golden era that had since been extinguished and consigned to historical records.

In December 1983, Buhari became head of state, following a bloodless coup that saw the overthrow of the then civilian president, Shehu Shagari, whose administration was riddled with allegations of massive corruption, impunity and socio-economic decay. The first decision that Buhari took as head of state and which signaled the direction of his administration was the appointment of Brigadier (later Major-General) Tunde Idiagbon as his Chief of Staff, or simply put, second-in-command. According to Buhari, he made the decision because Idiagbon was the only officer serving under him who used to return to the coffers of the Army; funds not spent at the end of every fiscal year. Besides, Idiagbon, like Buhari, was known to be a stern, stoic and highly principled man.

Thus set for the onerous task of governing a nation that needed urgent rescue from imminent collapse, Buhari started to systematically rebuild the nation's social-political and economic systems. He embarked on cutting back the excesses in national expenditure, expunging corruption from the nation's social ethics and shifting from mainly public sector employment to self-employment. He also encouraged import substitution industrialization based on the use of local materials and reduction of importation.

Let me try to break down some of his major achievements:

1. War Against Indiscipline (WAI)

This indeed was one of the most significant highlights of the Buhari/Idiagbon regime. Before the emergence of the government, Nigeria was in a dire state as far as ethics and etiquette were concerned. Corruption, crime and indiscipline were the order of the day in public places, offices, schools, agencies and institutions. Identifying these evils as the main hindrances to Nigeria's development and progress, Buhari and Idiagbon launched the nationwide "War Against Indiscipline" (WAI) campaign in March 1984.

> **The WAI campaign was aimed at instilling public morality, discipline, social order, civic responsibilities and promoting Nigerian nationalism.**

As usual, many initially thought the rules outlined in the campaign were mere jokes with empty threats. But as soon as the government began swift enforcement of punitive measures against violators, Nigerians quickly began to learn and grudgingly accept social behaviour that was the norm in other countries around the world. With the stern-looking officers of the WAI Brigades (set up in each state under the Ministry of Information and Culture) everywhere, queuing at bus stops and orderliness at other public places suddenly became a custom in Nigeria. Unruliness, littering, and urinating in public places suddenly became habits of the past as everyone knew the harsh punishments that would befall the culprits.

During that administration, regular environmental sanitation was a must for everyone. Violation attracted severe punishment. Punctuality at work, especially for public and civil servants was mandatory. Civil servants who failed to show up on time at work were humiliated and forced to do "frog jumps".

Indeed, the Buhari/Idigabon's anti-indiscipline campaign permeated every segment of the Nigerian society. Even in schools, examination malpractice, which has become the norm today, was counted as a serious crime. Any student over the age of 17 caught cheating in an exam would get 21 years in prison. Counterfeiting and arson could lead to the death penalty. Stealing or vandalizing public property attracted prompt arrest, prosecution and possible jail sentence. Expectedly, within a short time, Nigeria and Nigerians had become significantly transformed.

Sadly, as you look around today, things seem to have become even worse than they were before the Buhari-Idiagbon era. Today, indiscipline and indecency reign supreme in the Nigerian society. Almost every achievement of the WAI crusade seems to have been overturned.

Whether in the home, in schools, in public sectors, in the private sector, in government, on the road, in the hospital, or even in supposedly sacred houses (churches and mosques); daily events and reports suggest a society where morality and decency have almost become extinct.

Even while outside the country, many Nigerians are thoroughly undisciplined, shouting at airports, making noise inside the aircraft (or refusing to switch off phones or use seat belts), fighting over unnecessary things and destroying the country's image with criminal activities. In fact, things have reached such unimaginable proportions that indiscipline has become synonymous with smartness. The root cause of this, as I have repeatedly pointed out, is the corrupt value system of the populace.

2. Prosecution and Jailing of Corrupt Politicians

Buhari wasted no time in addressing widespread allegations of corruption against many members of the previous government of Shagari. Military tribunals were set up to try ministers and governors that had been accused of embezzling public funds. These tribunals were chaired by military officers and had the power to impose massive prison sentences. Even when the Nigerian Bar Association barred its member lawyers from participating in the tribunals, Buhari and Idiagbon still pressed on with the tribunals. Several prominent politicians were convicted of various corruption charges and given massive prison sentences. The government jailed as many as 600 corrupt politicians and businessmen and refused to release them until their loot was recovered.

Till today, the era of Buhari and Idiagbon is acclaimed as the first and only time that Nigerian public officials were tried, and held accountable for their actions in office. So determined was the government to prosecute corrupt politicians and recover their loots that when one of Shagari's ministers, Umaru Dikko, who was alleged to have stolen billions of Naira, fled to the U.K. and the British government refused to extradite him; the Buhari/Idiagbon government tried to kidnap and bring him to justice in Nigeria. Even though the attempt was eventually foiled, the determination of the government sent a strong message to other corrupt public officials that there would be no hiding place for them.

Interestingly, the Buhari-Idiagbon government was not blindly punitive in any way. For instance, when 250 politicians from all over the country were declared by investigators not to have any case to answer, the government ordered all of them released. These included Adamu Ciroma, the late Ikemba of Nnewi, Dim Odumegwu Ojukwu, Audu Innocent Ogbeh, and many others.

Sadly again, as soon as the next government took over, even the successfully prosecuted and jailed looters were released in droves.

3. Defiance of IMF and its ruinous dictates

From the beginning of his government, Buhari made it very clear that he would not be doing any business with the International Monetary Fund (IMF), especially when the organization asked him to devalue the Naira by 60%. He spurned their loans which are in reality, booby traps (the next government would later gladly take them to the peril of the nation). Buhari instead, advocated for barter and direct countertrade with Brazil and other nations of the Third World. He was more interested in bartering oil for technology, spare parts and raw materials. Naturally, that pitched him against the West but he was undeterred.

Other achievements of the Buhari government included his refusal to raise fuel price. In fact, he is said to be the only Nigerian leader who did not touch the prices of petroleum products from the time of Gowon's regime. He also significantly minimized oil bunkering and when bunkered oil was seized, he used it to get relevant commodities, equipment and machinery, using the counter trade policy. The latter measure ensured that Nigeria was exporting even above the OPEC quota.

Beyond that, his government greatly reduced the nation's inflation rate (from 40% to 3%), trade deficit and national debt. He prohibited borrowing by state governments (a practice that has become terribly abused in recent times). He diversified the economy, focusing more on agriculture. He specifically gave priority to the importation of raw materials and spare parts that were needed for agriculture and industry. He also stabilized the Naira. One of the ways he did this was to suddenly change the colour of the Naira to stop illegal printing and theft. It was a mechanism to boost confidence in the currency and slamming the door against looters that had billions of the currency stashed outside Nigeria.

Very importantly, Buhari was reported as the only ex-President of the country not living in opulence because his anti-corruption crusade was a transparent one that saw him being at the forefront. In fact, when he declared his assets recently, as the new civilian President, the entire amount in his bank account was around 30 million naira (150,000 USD). Even his second-in-command, who had never held a major political position, had something much higher.

But what did Buhari and Idiagbon get for all their transformational efforts and transparent government? They were forcefully removed from office by people who were terrified that the sweeping effects of their anti-corruption efforts would get to them. On August 27th 1985 (while Idiagbon was out of the country on a religious visit to Saudi Arabia), Buhari was overthrown in a military coup led by his Chief of Army Staff, Major-General Ibrahim Babangida.

So you see the point I have tried to establish so far. While the two leaders I have discussed in this chapter were busy thinking and working for the progress of the nation, the people under them were having different plans, due to retrogressive value systems. What's even worse is the fact that as soon as the Nigerian populace heard the news of the overthrow of Buhari/Idiagbon government, millions of Nigerians trooped to the streets jumping and dancing. The general thought among the people was that now they no longer had to queue up to enter buses, they no longer had to wake up early to go to work or be required to abide by other disciplinary measures of the Buhari/Idiagbon government.

This again is a clear demonstration of the fact that when God blesses a nation with a remnant leader, who has the right value systems, the people must also undergo a thorough re-orientation in their value systems. By the way, that is what the Buhari government tried to do. Unfortunately, the corrupt value system of the people was so strong that they rather rejoiced when a leader more like them in the person of General Babagida took over the realm of authority. A government is only a reflection of the value system of its people. When the Nigerian people rejoiced that the Buhari government was overthrown, while welcoming with joy the corrupt government of Babangida, it tells us the whole story of where we are as a people and as a nation. This definitely must change before any significant progress could be recorded in our nation.

As should be expected, the consequences on the nation were terrible. The reversal of the good works of the leaders, the release of criminals who should be in jail, the return to the old ways of indiscipline and impunity, and the ripple negative effects on the economic, political and social lives of the populace.

GOLDEN TRUTHS
FROM CHAPTER 6

- Even though leaders are often products and reflections of their environments, there are a few exceptions.

- Nigeria, with a fundamental problem of wrong value systems, has surprisingly been blessed with a few of these remnant leaders in the past.

- General Murtala Muhammed and General Muhammadu Buhari (as a military ruler) respectively proved to be messianic leaders, but their tenures were abruptly terminated.

- General Murtala was assassinated in office, while Buhari was ousted through a coup

7

REMNANT LEADERS WITH UNSUSTAINED LEGACIES

A concerted effort to preserve our heritage is a vital link to our cultural, educational, aesthetic, inspirational, and economic legacies - all of the things that quite literally make us who we are.

—**Steve Berry**

In this chapter, I will be discussing the second category of remnant leaders. These are those who were able to successfully govern in Nigeria without being rejected or overthrown. This second category includes the government of Chief Obafemi Awolowo in the western part of Nigerian, on the one hand; and on the other hand was the government of President Olusegun Obasanjo in his second coming as a civilian President. Sadly, though, as I will be showing you, their great achievements and exceptional legacies could not be sustained by the people coming after them due to the same problems of wrong attitudes and corrupt value systems of majority of the citizens.

However, before I fully explore the details of the achievements of this second category of remnant leaders, I would like to again restate what I said in the previous chapter, that no matter how rebellious a people are as in the case of the Israelites, God knows how to raise up a Moses.

The people of Israel were renowned for being probably the most stubborn and stiffnecked people according to God's definition. Yet, God had a remnant leader for them in the person of Moses, so also can we say about Nigeria. Throughout the history of the nation, we have had examples of such remnant leaders. However, no matter how gifted these leaders are, regardless of what type of qualities or character and virtues they possess, if they do not first of all change the value system of the populace, their efforts and achievements will end up being an exercise in futility. This was clearly shown to us in the history of Moses and the children of Israel.

Now, let's briefly look at the achievements and legacies of Chief Obafemi Awolowo and Chief Olusegun Obasanjo.

CHIEF OBAFEMI AWOLOWO

Awolowo was so different from his contemporaries that even they, his contemporaries, feared and respected his sense of thought, direction, competence and foresight. Among them, he was viewed as a prophet. He acted with great foresight and wisdom, such that some people even referred to him as a prophet. He was a man who had the rare ability to see today from yesterday and tomorrow from today.

The first great achievement that he recorded in the western region of Nigeria was the reformation he brought to the local government system of the western region. He brought the level of the civil service at par with the European countries. Awolowo was an extremely good judge of men's qualities. He assembled a very efficient team of ministers that achieved outstanding feats. The government of Chief Obafemi Awolowo was full of a history of "firsts".

> His team of ministers was so good that almost everything they did was the first of its kind in Africa. At the same time, Awolowo managed to assemble a civil service that was acclaimed to be the best civil service system in Africa.

Let's examine some of his other achievements in his years in office between 1954 and 1959.

1. First Free Primary Education in Africa

His government introduced and successfully implemented the first free primary education program in Africa. If not because of such a program, millions of Nigerians especially those who lived in the western part of the nation would still be in their father's farms today. Most Nigerian citizens could not afford to send their children to school, much less paying for their tuition.

Awolowo changed the destiny of millions of Nigerians, thanks to his program. This program of free primary education later became a question of embarrassment to the federal government of Nigeria such that the Obasanjo government in September 1976 had to ask for the help of Awolowo to help implement the free education to the whole of Nigeria.

We could therefore say that all Nigerians benefited and are still benefiting from the life and foresight of Obafemi Awolowo. Even though this is indirect, it is obvious that the federal government introduced the free primary education to all Nigerians, because they were first provoked by the success of Awolowo's government.

Till today the western part of Nigeria is regarded as a more educated segment of Nigeria than others. This was in sharp contrast to what obtained in other parts of the nation, where parents sent their children for apprenticeship to learn trade and skills. The western part of Nigeria is home to the Yorubas and they mostly benefited from Awolowo's rule and policies. It must also be stated here that Awolowo never made any exceptions to citizens of western region when he provided his services and benefits to the people. They were given to all who lived in the western part of the nation, regardless of their origin. So, if an Igbo person lived in Ibadan or Benin, they benefited from the policies of Chief Awolowo. So also was a Hausa person, Idoma person or whoever they might be.

Still on education, records have it that when he came to office there were close to 43,000 pupils enrolled in schools in all of western Nigeria in 1954. In the next one year, he had increased the number by 77% enrollment; while the number of secondary school was increased from 46 to 139. Then he introduced new sets of secondary schools called secondary modern schools. He built an additional 363 of those. By the time he left office in 1959, they were enrolling over a million pupils from 43,000.

He also gave post-secondary scholarship awards annually to exceptional students. Additionally, Chief Awolowo started the famous University of Ife, later to be renamed after him as Obafemi Awolowo University.

2. First Free Medical Service in Nigeria

Growing up as a young boy in western Nigeria, as little as our community was (my village consisted of about 40 huts), Awolowo's government made sure that we had a dispensary, like a little local village hospital to give medical services. It was meant to give medical services to all other villages. From my recollection growing up, there was always a dispensary for every five villages no matter how small they were. Besides that, we had medical staff and workers coming to every home on a weekly basis to check the quality of water that was being drunk in every household. They checked the reservoirs and water collectors. They gave services and recommendations. They made sure that both adults and children lived in a hygienic environment. Even though this was about 10 years after Awolowo had left office, the system remained in place for another fifteen years after he left office before everything began to crumble.

The level and standard of maintenance of the medical service were so high that they became a source of envy and a point of reference to all developing countries that were just gaining their independence all over Africa and the rest of the world. Awolowo's program of free medical service was so comprehensive that it covered and provided free medical services to children from birth to 18 years old. Interestingly, this was before the oil boom of the seventies. He was so industrious and innovative that he generated all his income from within his western region. His government was absolutely self-sufficient.

3. First Television Station in Africa

Most Nigerians will find it difficult to believe that Nigeria had a television station before countries like South Africa, Egypt, Ethiopia, and Algeria yet this is a fact of history. Chief Awolowo established the first TV station in Africa; and if this is not shocking enough to you, then get this: Nigeria had a television station before 98% of the countries of the world! When people in France did not know what a television station was, Nigerians already had it. So revolutionary was the government of Chief Awolowo that

149

he was not competing with any country in Africa or any other developing country. His standard of competition only ranked with the best and leading countries of Europe.

Today, France is the second biggest economy in Europe; it has since left Nigeria behind. How did this happen? Simple: when Chief Awolowo left the scene, the people who came to replace him did not carry the same value system that he carried. Therefore, his achievements and accomplishments could not be maintained, not to talk of them being continued or improved upon.

When a nation is gifted with a leader and yet the whole country remains at a lower level of value systems, those who come after him will destroy and ruin his legacies rather than maintaining them.

4. First Modern Sports Facility in Nigeria

Nigeria never knew any modern or sophisticated sports complex till Awolowo decided to break that jinx. He decided that his capital city of Ibadan was worthy of its own Wembley stadium and he made sure he did it by constructing the famous Liberty Stadium of Ibadan. It took him only one year to build. He started on September 30, 1959 and opened it on September 30, 1960. The stadium has a sitting capacity of 40,000 with additional facilities and indoor sports hall for 1000 spectators.

Unfortunately, unlike Wembley which has since undergone modern constructions and upgrading, Liberty Stadium has suffered the fate of all other modern facilities in Nigeria plagued by lack of management and abandonment. Anybody who visits Ibadan today will not believe that Liberty Stadium used to be one of the best stadiums in the whole world as at the time it was built. It was an ultra-modern sports complex of its time.

This again confirms the truth that when the pot is not cleansed, it will be difficult to keep on producing leaders of such caliber as

Chief Obafemi Awolowo.

Unfortunately, things are so bad in our nation today that even the ultra-modern stadium in Abuja that was constructed during the government of Obasanjo which is only a few years old could not be maintained because of our lack of maintenance culture, yet it was one of the best stadiums in the world when it was constructed. Until the whole value system of the general citizenry changes there will be no progress no matter the effort put in by their leaders.

5. The First Minimum Wage Policy in Nigeria

Awolowo was so good and meticulous that he almost never failed in his predictions especially in matters of the economy. Before coming to power in the western region on October 1, 1954, he had promised that, once elected, the first thing he was going to do was to double the wages of the workers. He then went ahead to make all the calculations and preparations to implement this policy. So conscientious was he that he fulfilled his promise the very first month he came into power.

Throughout his administration, Awolowo made sure that workers in western Nigeria were well paid. This caused mass migration of other Nigerians from other parts of the country to the west, because western Nigerian workers were being paid double of what workers in other parts of Nigeria were earning.

6. Farm Settlements

In his efforts to generate income for his government, Chief Awolowo embarked on massive agricultural projects. He embarked on radical and revolutionary projects that brought sustenance to the economy and the lives of people of the western part of Nigeria. He bought over large pieces of land and territories and converted them into agricultural settlements where he moved able-bodied men that were not employed. He gave such good incentives to young families to move to these farm settlements that people were moving into them en masse just to do agriculture.

Various plantations that he started covered over 20,000 acres of land. Such settlements included the Apoja oil palm and the Sagamu rubber estates. Awolowo also started a cattle ranch as in the American culture. One cattle ranch in Ogun State covered over 26, 000 acres of land. He also had a rubber processing factory in Benin, and a large fruit canning factory in Ibadan. He constructed the first ultra-modern cement company called West African Portland Cement Company. He started Lafia Rest House (now Lafia Hotel) in Ibadan, which was an ultra-modern hotel facility. He also started Premier Hotel, which was a five-star hotel as at then. It will be considered a three-star hotel today because of lack of maintenance.

7. Western Development Corporation

Awolowo was such a visionary that he envisaged a developed Nigeria. Since he was only in charge of the western part of the country as a premier, he started Western Development Corporation that was supposed to see into a rapid development of that part of the nation. He tasked the establishment with the responsibility of bringing about unprecedented development to the people of western Nigeria. They were to make sure that western Nigeria achieved such a quick level of development so as to catch up with the rest of the world in the shortest possible time.

To make sure that money was not an issue, he raised financial corporations to deal with raising money to finance the projects and ideas that people would be coming up with. His government built roads, constructed highways, and even a university within the five years of his governance.

Chief Obafemi Awolowo so much wanted to change the

destiny and lifestyle of his people that he was determined to bring the people of western Nigeria to live in more modern structures rather than in huts and mud houses that they were used to, as of the time of his government. To achieve this, he started the Western Nigerian Housing Corporation. The sole responsibility of this corporation was to improve the living conditions of western Nigerians.

One of the first major accomplishments of the corporation was the construction of the 350-acre Bodija Housing Estate in Ibadan. To date, it is still the biggest and most respected estate in Ibadan 50 years later. A similar estate was built in Lagos as part of the western government of Awolowo. In Lagos alone, he built the 750-acre Ikeja Housing Estate which is 2 times bigger than the Ibadan estate. The Ikeja estate became a whole industrial estate for companies and industries that provided job, employment, services and a booming economic atmosphere in the western Nigeria. 550 acres were used for housing while 200 acres were used to build industries.

You wonder what other leaders after him have done? If a leader could do this in five years and in 50 years other leaders have not been able to surpass what he did, it means that there is a discrepancy in value systems. If a country is to sustain and advance the level of progress and development achieved through a certain leader, the same value systems that such a remnant leader upholds must be cultivated in all the citizens of the land.

8. Trading Companies and Businesses

The government of Obafemi Awolowo understood the need to continually generate finances for the needs of his government. He knew that internally generated revenues were the only way forward. Thank God that, at that time, there was no distribution of oil money which Nigeria later adopted. Every region needed to generate its own money.

Chief Awolowo embarked on this task aggressively. He exploited every possible means to create enough wealth for his people. For this cause, he promoted the WEMA Bank and National Bank of Nigeria which were later merged together, but has since been mismanaged by the succeeding generation. He also started the Nigeria Insurance Corporation Limited to give comfort and security to businesses and individuals.

Awolowo continued to adapt into his government every major achievement that had been recorded in the western world. With the help of Dutch companies form the Netherlands, Awolowo effectively exploited the landscape of western Nigeria to create wealth. For this to succeed, he started Gravil Enbethoven and Co. to convert the stones, hills, and mountains of western Nigeria into sources of income, both for roads and for house constructions.

Awolowo was mindful to ensure that the wealth of his region was not confined to a few individuals. So he started a corporate bank where middle income farmers and low income earners could go to get credit and loans for their businesses. Awolowo created a lot of wealth by encouraging businessmen and farmers to form themselves into cooperative societies. As a result the number of cooperative societies in western Nigeria rose from 564 to close to 1000 just in four years of his government between 1954 and 1958.

9. Micro Finance Scheme

Even though the idea of micro financing is a new concept which was only started in the nineties by Bangladesh's Mohamed Yunus, yet in his ingenuity, Chief Awolowo had started his own type of micro financing to empower his people back in the fifties. He would invite enterprising individuals and challenge them to go start their businesses, telling them that money would not be an issue. He provided advances to farmers to increase their productivity and buy crops and seeds. He made loans of five to fifty pounds available to farmers.

This idea of giving small amounts of money to enterprising individuals is the whole concept behind micro financing which is lauded all over the world as a new concept. But, indeed, this concept was operated and used successfully by Awolowo in the fifties. More than that, he also saw the need for foreign currency earning since that was the only way a nation could get money for its produce. He gave money to farmers especially to produce for export. That was the only way to maintain balance of trade and stay competitive. He provided the money especially to those farmers who wanted to produce for the international market. When the farmers complained about pests destroying their produce, he provided money for them to buy pesticides.

Such was Awolowo's ingenuity and brilliance that when the Nigerian Federal government ran into trouble in executing the civil war with Biafra, the then head of state General Gowon had to fetch Awolowo from his temporary political retirement to come and manage the war time economy. He performed so excellently that Nigeria never needed to borrow one penny throughout the whole war. Today, without war, Nigeria is heavily burdened with debt. I think it is only logical that the Nigerian currency till today carries the name that was given to it by Chief Obafemi Awolowo.

Now, despite all the above mentioned achievements and accomplishments of Chief Obafemi Awolowo, it is shocking to go to western Nigeria today and see how derelict the region is. Even though people still get educated but, as with Moses and the children of Israel, as long as the value system of the people remains unchanged, no matter the amount of prosperity they enjoy or the education they get, that "pot" will keep on producing according to its corrupt value system.

In the Old Testament, the personal qualities and values of

Moses did not automatically transfer to the general populace. For this to happen, there must be a deliberate effort to release those value system upon the general population. These values must be promoted in the schools, media, and entertainment and in all government agencies. If that is not done, the same thing that happened after the departure of Chief Awolowo will keep on happening in our nation. Such is the fate of societies that don't systematically emulate and propagate the value system of the remnant leaders.

MICHAEL IHEONUKARA OKPARA

DR. M .I. Okpara can be said to be the man that laid a solid industrial base for the development of eastern Nigeria for the then period and for future generations. He was a political leader and Premier of Eastern Nigeria during the First Republic, from 1959 to 1966. At 39, he was the nation's youngest Premier. He was a strong advocate of what he called "pragmatic socialism" and believed that agricultural reform was crucial to the ultimate success of Nigeria. If leaders after him had kept to the path which he took in bringing a revolution to his people, it is safe to say that Nigeria's economy and development will be far better than it is today.

1. The Construction Of The Nkalagu Cement Company And Other Power Plants

According to Igbo Focus Uk, He pioneered the construction of the Nkalagu cement company and this move is one that can be considered as a bold, decisive, courageous and sensible business decision. He bought the government shared interest which was to be disposed of.

It was inconceivable to Dr. Okpara that such a strategic

industry located in Nkalagu, a few miles from Enugu, would be allowed to be acquired by a British consortium. The political implications of that move would be catastrophic to the industrial and developmental interest of his government. Therefore the Federal Government interests were substantially bought over by the Okpara government and sold to the ordinary people of Eastern Nigeria.

In like manner was the establishment of the Niger-gas plant and Niger steel industry, all in Emene. This move challenged the federal government to embark on a bold industrial steel production policy which led to the establishment of Ajaokuta, Warri, Oshogbo and Katsina steel plants.

2. The International Market And Industrial Growth

Furthermore, to open up the vast opportunities of an International Market, Dr. Okpara's government planned and executed the completion of the Onitsha International Market which, today, has spread over a sprawling area attracting traders from many cities in Nigeria and the ECOWAS region. Added to this, was the building and inauguration of the Pepsi Cola plant in Onitsha by the Eastern Nigeria Development Corporation (ENDC). In addition, there was plan for the establishment of a textile factory which was on the drawing board and actually took off after the Nigeria/Biafra Civil conflict with a combination of government and private interests running the outfit. Also the administration planned the building of a motor manufacturing plant in the region to enable Nigeria to join the league of automobile producers as well as provide employment for Nigerians.

The industrial floodgate was really thrown open with the establishment of the Shoe Industry at Owerri, the Aba Textile Mill with industrial gas piped from Port-Harcourt. The Modern

Ceramic Industry came on stream producing primary sanitary wares, bath tubes as well as tiles, while the Metallic Industry was also in the offing for the production of small machine tools.

In Port Harcourt, Dr. Michael Okpara's visionary acumen blossomed in the establishment and development of a vast Industrial Estate which, to this day, remains the heart beat and bulwark of industrial development in Port Harcourt, Rivers State. The Trans-Amadi Layout was, and still remains, an unbeatable venture in vision and business savvy. Also the Alfa pioneer plant was to be built for plywood production in line with the government's policy of massive industrialization. As part of the Vision, model warehouses were built and solid roads were laid out with drains. Electricity, water, gas pipe lines, environment-friendly installations were put in place and industries just moved in and commenced production. The result was that the flourishing Michelin Tyre Factory was in full bloom. The Glass Factory, established by the ENDC, was in full production with the Trans-Amadi layout established by the administration not too far away from that area. There was also the Coconut Plantation in Bonny Island owned by the ENDC.

ENDC also took over some of the Bulk Oil Plant premises to establish a flourishing boatyard, manufacturing some power fired engine passenger boats for use between, Igwe-nga, now renamed Ikot Abasi, in Akwa-Ibom State, and the historic and famous king Jaja of Opobo Town. No part of Eastern Nigeria was neglected or excluded from the industrial blitz.

3. Tourism And Hospitality

As part of tourism Development efforts of the Dr. Okpara Government, apart from building the two exquisite Hotel Presidential in Enugu, and Port Harcourt, run by Hotel management experts from Europe, a network of Old Catering

Rest Houses were rehabilitated and rekitted to update their services. In 1964, new catering Rest Houses located in various strategic areas of Eastern Nigeria were built and run in Ogoja, Owerri and Uyo.

4. Health Insurance Vision

Dr. Okpara, in his very intuitive character, outlined a road map he would wish to see in place in Nigeria. On 4th April 1981; Dr. Okpara noted that the Medical and Health problems facing Nigeria is how to take the increasing modern services to the rural areas.

Dr. Okpara, undertook a public enlightenment campaign to explain in details the possible forms of the Health Insurance Scheme which he recommended, and other forms of social welfare insurance to include unemployment insurance and old age pensions.

Then, Dr. Okpara expressed the view and advised that, perhaps the West German model which was based on a Health Insurance Scheme in which the governments, the corporations and individuals, contributed towards the medical care of all the citizens. He then recommended that a presidential commission should be put together and empowered to study the problem in all its ramifications and make appropriate and workable recommendations within six months from April, nineteen eighty one. Certainly, the current health insurance scheme being applied in the country mostly among federal civil servants and a few states that have adopted the scheme point to the fact that Dr. Okpara was visionary.

5. Infrastructural Development Efforts

His administration gave priority to infrastructural development as many rural roads were constructed throughout the region to the point that in 1996, Eastern region was acclaimed as having the best network of roads in Africa. The whole essence was to accelerate commerce and evacuate farm produce from the rural area to make industries to thrive. Also there was high speed development of social services as many communities enjoyed electricity and water supply because they were readily mobilized to contribute funds to project.

6. Educational Sector

In the area of education, the sector achieved a quantum leap as primary and secondary schools grew in large number with voluntary agencies and churches actively engaged in the establishment of schools leading to an appreciable expansion in knowledge with the government liberalizing local and overseas scholarship. Consequently both voluntary schools and government schools existed side with each working with commitment to put education in the front seat.

7. Outstanding Agricultural Policies And Programmes

Under his regime which has been aptly described as the most radical, progressive and result-oriented, agriculture was giving an outstanding position as the period witnessed real agrarian revolution and economic expansion. Indeed, agriculture was the center piece of his development policy, using the Eastern Nigerian Development Corporation ENDC as instrument.

It is indisputable that what is now referred to an agrarian revolution and economic development by succeeding administrations were first started by the Okara administrations in Eastern Nigerian. Dr. Opkara did not only talk of agriculture, he put flesh and blood into it with relentless interest and aggressive policies which culminated into a rapid social, economic and industrial transformation. These efforts still and will remain a monumental tribute to him and many generations to come, as despite callous neglect and abandonment by successive regimes evidence of his achievements still abound.

As a deliberate approach for success, innovative farm settlements patterned after the famous Israeli Kibutz were set up in five towns, Igborariam in now Anambra state, and the one located in now Ebonyi State, Ulonna North and South in now Abia state, Uzo-Uwani in now Enugu state and Ohaji in now Imo state. The idea was to ensure that model farms properly managed by experts were established to train young school leavers who worked in the settlement and ran their own farms inside the estates based on the experience they acquired and were supervised by the farm management. The product ranged from rice, oil palm to rubber.

Sadly, at the end of the Nigeria/Biafra Civil War, some of the farm settlements were remodeled or sold out rightly or privatized, while many were simple abandoned and to allowed to waste. For example Adapalm at Ohaji in Imo state, was remodeled into thriving vast commercial oil palm plantation but which has been mismanaged.

In the area of protein production, it was Dr. Okpara's accepted agricultural policy to massively produce poultry product for which purpose, an expert Afro American, Mr. Davies was recruited to develop poultry productions in Abakaliki. Chicken broilers, day old chicks, old layers, and egg were available on a very massive scale for distribution throughout the Region. The People were mobilized and agriculture made conscious, available on a very massive scale for distribution throughout the Region. Then public servants were encouraged, and persuaded, to grow their own poultry for family consumption in their back-yard farms. Almost every home produces all the egg and broilers consumed by the family and the surplus made available for sale. It was Dr. Opkara's passion that the population should be well fed. In fact, the slogan then was "grow your own chicken and egg."

To show the extent to which the policy yielded enormous dividend, Egg marketing and Distribution Task Force comprising the Ministry of Agriculture, Local Government, Co-operative Department of Ministry of Commerce, Ministry of Education, and Eastern Nigeria Development Corporation, was set up with a Secretary from the premier's Office given the mandate to organize immediate egg collection centers in all local Government Areas. Cold rooms were built in convenient centers to receive the egg and organize logistics for distribution of eggs. For ease of distribution, the Education Ministry was asked to feed every student in the secondary schools in the Region that had dormitory accommodation, two eggs a week! Unfortunately this grand program, no longer exists with the inception of succeeding administrations.

CHIEF OLUSEGUN OBASANJO

Unsurprisingly, what happened to the achievements and legacies of Awolowo also befell those of another remnant leader, Chief Olusegun Obasanjo, who was Nigeria's civilian president between 1999 and 2007. Stern in discipline and sagacious in decision-making, Chief Olusegun Obasanjo proved to be a befitting leader for a peculiar country like Nigeria. He took many drastic decisions and introduced sweeping reforms that shook the entire country, leaving holistic transformation in its wake.

One cannot forget so soon that it was through Chief Obasanjo's economic policies that the Nigerian banking sector was overhauled and the banks in the country were consolidated. The capital adequacy requirements for banks were ruthlessly raised from N2 billion to N25 billion, making many people to wonder how the plan would succeed. However, in just about 20 months later, the policy – and the chain of recapitalizations and mergers it heralded – transformed Nigeria's banking sector for the better and strengthened the country's overall economic stability. It was also under his regime that Nigeria became a beneficiary of the debt relief packages from the Paris and London clubs. These packages ensured that the heavy financial burden that Nigeria bore at its yearly budgets to service debts from past governments was relieved. For the payment of $12 billion of the principal, Nigeria was forgiven its debts totaling $32 billion.

Even after the huge sums paid to the Paris and London clubs, the Obasanjo's administration's astuteness and judiciousness ensured that the country had enough in its coffers, at home and abroad. Nigeria's foreign reserves grew from $4 billion in 1999 to $43.5 billion as at December 2006. In fact, during his regime, the country's economy grew at an impressive rate of 6.5% from 2003 as against 2.8% in the 1990s; the inflation rate also dropped from 26% to 9% (December 2006), and the Naira significantly appreciated against international currencies.

Very significantly, privatization/deregulation was a major policy thrust of the administration of President Olusegun Obasanjo. He established the National Council on Privatization (NCP) to see to the privatization of several public enterprises that had become worthless white elephants. The most enduring legacy of that move is the transformation of the telecommunication sector that had been moribund over the years. By the end of Obasanjo's tenure in 2007, the total number of telephone lines in the country had risen from mere 450,000 to 38 million. Now, almost every Nigerian has a GSM line. Additionally, the liberalization of the supply side of petroleum products and the liberalization of the capital market were prominent features of Chief Obasanjo's economic policies.

Before the emergence of the Obasanjo government, there was no black man that controlled a total wealth of a billion dollars on the African continent. Obasanjo's government changed that. Even though most of his countrymen will attack and criticize him for raising up billionaires in the likes of Aliko Dangote, Femi Otedola, Mike Adenuga, Jimoh Ibrahim, Jim Ovia, Cecilia Ibru, Chris Uba, Andy Uba, Emeka Offor, Tony Elumelu, Erastus Akingbola and Abdulsamad Rabiu, to mention a few of those who benefited from Obasanjo's government, history tells us that without such wealthy individuals, there is no way strong industries could be established; and without strong industries, there is no strong economy. Most of these people who made their fortunes during Obasanjo's regime went on to become captains of industry, not just in Nigeria but in the whole continent of Africa.

It is only thanks to the emergence of such strong and powerful billionaires that Nigeria can now be mentioned in economic terms on the world stage. Several Nigerian banks now rank in the top 1000 banks of the world. Thanks to this single policy of the Obasanjo government. It is believed Nigeria will soon become one of the largest producers of cement in the world through the company of Africa's richest man, Aliko Dangote.

The vision of the Obasanjo regime was to raise up multinational companies that would be able to provide foreign exchange earnings for the country through industrial products rather than through raw materials as the country had been prone to do so far.

Obasanjo was also ruthless in his fight against corruption. To begin with, his regime recognized the indispensability of the concept and practice of transparency, accountability and the rule of law in sustaining the market economy. This dimension led to the enacting of the law that set up the Economic and Financial Crimes Commission (EFCC). This commission is probably the most important creation of Obasanjo's government. The fear of the EFCC was the beginning of wisdom for many public office holders, as well as fraudsters among ordinary citizens. During his tenure, a lot of high profile cases were tried and people who had been thought untouchable were jailed.

I must also point to Obasanjo's impact on the health sector, especially the resuscitation and empowerment of the National Agency for Food and Drug Administration and Control (NAFDAC). Before his regime, Nigerians had been at the mercy of charlatans who specialized in manufacturing and importing adulterated drugs and foods into the country. Even though NAFDAC that was supposed to check these activities had been in existence long before then, many Nigerians knew virtually nothing about it because the agency was as good as dead. However, as a reformer, Obasanjo had to appoint the late Prof. (Mrs) Dora Akunyili as Director General of the agency in 2001. Obasanjo had learnt about her uncommon act of honesty at the Petroleum Trust Fund, PTF, where she was serving as zonal secretary, and sent for her. That was the beginning of transformation for NAFDAC and great relief for Nigerians.

I could go on and on about the lofty achievements of that administration, but that's not my focus here. My focus, as I have repeatedly emphasized, is that Nigeria has had a few leaders who had done their best to improve the country but the attitude of the citizens has been a great challenge. Take for example the turn of events since the end of the Obasanjo's administration. What became of the EFCC and NAFDAC immediately he left? Any careful observer can testify that it was like the agencies became handicapped and comatose. The EFCC, in particular, appeared to have been immediately placed on powerful sedatives. Not until the coming of the the present administration of President Buhari did the agency awake from its protracted slumber and became fully active again.

Let's even look beyond that and consider the country's economy. Between the time Obasanjo left office and now, the huge foreign reserves the country once boasted of is reported to have been massively depleted by the succeeding governments. How about the debt burden that his government fought so hard to remove? Have things not become worse? In fact, it may shock you to know that as at July 2015, Nigeria's external debt stock profile had risen again to $10.3bn, according to the Debt Management Office (DMO) of the Federal Government.

Of course, I am not unaware of all the shortcomings of the Obasanjo regime. Still, I would give that government a pass mark, especially in comparison to all the other governments we have had at the federal level in this country. The facts and statistics listed above speak for themselves. Facts don't lie. No matter what we like or dislike about Chief Obasanjo's personality, we will be doing posterity a great wrong if we don't admit and give credit to whom it belongs. If we refuse to appreciate leaders who try their best on behalf of the nation then it will be hard to get good leaders because those with good intentions will be tempted to think it's worthless making costly sacrifices for the nation.

Nevertheless the main reason I decided to use the example of the Obasanjo government is that it is such a vivid picture to most Nigerians. In our own generation right before our own eyes, we can testify to how this principle of "corrupt pot" works. If the content of the pot has not been altered or changed, the emerging leaders after the good remnant leader will always frustrate his legacies. As I have hinted above, we saw that happen in the case of Obasanjo.

I am aware that Obasanjo himself tried his uttermost best to make sure that a man of character succeeded him as President, but the outcome of his efforts confirms the fact that it is not enough to just look for one exceptional remnant leader to succeed the other; the whole pot must first be reformed. When this happens, we would have no need to be searching for one exceptional person; we would have a whole lot of them. All this takes is for us to work on reforming the entire value system of our people. Nothing is more important than this in building a civilized society. We must deploy our media outfits, entertainment channels and school systems to propagate the right value systems of the nation we dream of. This is the most effective way to solve the Nigerian leadership problem.

Until the Nigerian citizenry imbibes a culture of responsibility and accountability, the emergence of a remnant leader may not have any lasting effect on the fate of the country. With the current attitude of many Nigerians, if we are to get a leader in the frame of Moses, the biggest problem he will face will not be that of the lack of vision or character, but how to change the people. Unfortunately, you can only force a horse to the stream; you cannot force it to drink water. It must voluntarily drink from the stream by itself.

What happens is that when the value system of the general populace remains unchanged, the subsequent leaders that come after a remnant leader will rather ruin, run down and undo all the achievements of the previous leader. Truth be told, as good and as great a leader as Awolowo was, his achievements and feats were eventually run down by those who have been ruling the western part of Nigeria after him. The reason?

You remember the analogy I gave earlier: if the pot, which is the pool from where we get our leaders, is dirty and corrupt, even though there might be an exception in the case of a remnant leader, yet if that pot is not cleansed, after the remnant leader leaves the stage, the pot will keep on producing other leaders that will reflect the state of the pot. These other leaders that will come after the remnant leader will reflect the corrupt nature of the pot; they will reflect the rottenness of the society and they will reflect the injustice and the oppression that is dominant in the society. In that case all the efforts, sacrifice and achievements of the remnant leader are brought to nothing.

A few years or decades after a remnant leader leaves the stage, his works are so ruined that there is normally no more remembrance of the great feats he had achieved. Unfortunately, we can say that is the situation with Nigeria as in the case of Awolowo in the western part of Nigeria and Obasanjo in his second rule as the president of Nigeria. That is exactly what has happened to us as a nation.

I cannot emphasise enough how urgently important the need for us as a nation to start an aggressive program of national reorientation in values and virtues. We need to redirect our people, we need to challenge our wrong value systems, we need to speak up the truth about what is wrong with our society, we need to face our failures and challenge our weaknesses.

We must stand up against our lack of good fundamental value systems upon which our nation is being built. From our kindergartens to the universities, we must begin to enforce and establish national value systems that will reflect the kind of nation we wish to see in the future.

It is wrong for us to only expect those values from our leaders because it will be too late by then. We must begin today by instilling the value systems we expect from our leaders into our kids in the kindergarten, in primary schools, in universities, now that they are still young - before they get into a place of authority. We must instill and nurture in all citizens of our country the right value system we dream about wherever they are, as students, workers, business people and professionals. All must carry and reflect the godly value systems that will make our nation proud.

You see, any leader who wants to do the right things would need to enforce those right principles upon the people. In so doing, people feel offended and they revolt. People want the benefits of change, but they themselves don't want to go through the process of change. They don't want to pay the price for the progress they wish to have. That is why they ask for great leaders who could pay that price for them, without him touching them. Once he begins to step on their toes, they call for his head. We have gone through that many times in our short history as a nation in Nigeria.

Anytime the right leader comes to a country, the people of the land would most often revolt and fight his government. Why? Because any government that comes to do the right thing, would call for a change in the lifestyle of the people, which invariably results in conflict. The reason for the conflict is often because the same people who clamor for change and reform, always don't realize the price they themselves would have to pay for the change they are clamoring for.

The point I am trying to make therefore, is that while Nigeria needs a leader with the character and charisma of Moses, he can only succeed if the citizens change their mindset and rise up to the challenge of responsible citizenship. The leader's job is to point the way forward, but it is the duty of the people to follow. The leader leads the way; he stirs the ship of the nation based on the vision he has seen, towards the set objective. The role of the leader is just to inspire, to encourage and influence the people to move forward. The leader cannot do more than lead the people. He cannot do more than dream and communicate the dream to the people. He cannot force the people to follow accordingly.

> **With the current attitude of many Nigerians, if we are to get a leader in the frame of Moses, the biggest problem he will face will not be that of the lack of vision or character, but how to change the people.**

It is therefore my desire to use this medium to call on all well-meaning Nigerians to begin an aggressive campaign for moral reorientation in our people. The government alone cannot do this. This is a task for every responsible citizen. We must have pressure groups, non-governmental organizations that will carry values of righteousness and godliness into every nuke and cranny of our country. If this is done, the Nigerian entity will never need to worry about who we elect into political offices, because once the pot is clean the content from it will reflect the nature of that pot. Once our people become a virtous people, only godly leaders will emerge to lead us.

At this juncture, I hope to make mention of my next book which is going to be on what values great nations build their countries. The book, which will be called "National Greatness Starts from Here" will reflect on the values for greatness of several nations including Nigeria. Watch out!

GOLDEN TRUTHS
FROM CHAPTER 7

- Obafemi Awolowo and Olusegun Obasanjo were two great leaders in Nigeria who were allowed to successfully complete their tenures of leadership.

- These two leaders accomplished several feats in national transformation and improvement in the living standards of the people.

- Sadly, however, most of their legacies were soon mismanaged, overturned or destroyed by their successors with the collaboration of the citizens.

- These examples further show that without the citizens imbibing noble values of discipline, selflessness, patriotism and sound maintenance culture, among others, even the best efforts of a great leader will not have lasting impact on the nation

8

CITIZENS AS DRIVERS OF NATIONAL DEVELOPMENT

The efforts of the government alone will never be enough. In the end the people must choose and the people must help themselves."

—John F. Kennedy

As has already been established in this book, in a democracy, which has become the benchmark for all progressive governments and nations, real power for change, growth and development resides with the people.

Even from a strictly logical perspective, it stands to reason that since the government consists of a few number of individuals, compared to the generality of the populace, the collective decision of the citizens will have more impact and influence in determining the fortune and fate of a nation.

To this end, I have decided to devote this chapter to highlighting the contributions of selected citizens of Nigeria who I think provide good examples for every one of us to follow in our quest to experience and enjoy the Nigeria of our dreams.

> **These exemplary men and women have individually chosen to distinguish themselves by realizing that the ultimate key for national transformation is the individual decision of each citizen to imbibe good values, demonstrate godly character, and commit themselves to contributing a quota in whichever way they can.**

Thus, they are working assiduously and developing unique strategies to enlighten their fellow citizens, improve their communities and transform their nation.

These people too could have chosen the pathway of the complaining majority, who are always waiting for the government to change for good so that the course of their lives and the nation can be changed. Rather, they have individually chosen to be agents of solution by embracing progressive values and virtues, discovering and developing their potentials, as well as sacrificially using their abilities to improve the circumstances of their fellow citizens and the lots of their communities.

Let's learn from them.

1. Fela Durotoye

Fela Durotoye is one man with both the vision and the passion to see a new Nigeria, where morality, accountability, stability and prosperity will prevail in every sphere. A renowned nation building strategist, he describes his life's passion as "building people into super achievers, organisations into global players and nations into desirable societies!" This noble desire has been the driving force of his life and the watchword of his various outreaches. So committed is he to the vision of a new Nigeria that he has set the audacious goal of "building Nigeria into a most desirable nation to live in by 31st December 2025".

And to show that he means business and not merely daydreaming, he has established the GEMSTONE Nation Builder Network which has the mandate to identify, attract, empower, equip, motivate and mentor "Nation Builders" who will be committed to the process of building Nigeria into the world's most desirable nation to live in by December 31st 2025. He has also developed the Nation Builder's Creed, with which he is re-orientating, equipping and empowering all within his circle of influence towards the realization of the totally-transformed Nigeria dream.

I will reproduce the content of the creed here because I believe it contains crucial principles and values which every one of us can imbibe and demonstrate in turning our nation around for good:

Mine is a Generation that is Empowered, Motivated and Stirred to Operate with Natural Excellence. This day, I hereby commit to live an exemplary lifestyle of leadership and excellence and to do all within my power to transform my country into the most desirable nation to live in.

To this end, I will:
- Make A Positive Impact On Everyone I Meet and Everywhere I Go
- Be A Solution Provider And Not A Part Of The Problem To Be Solved
- Be A Role Model Worthy Of Emulation
- Be My Best In All I Do, Particularly The Things I Am

Naturally Good At
- Do The Right Thing At All Times Regardless Of Who Is Doing The Wrong Thing
- Value Time And Make The Best Use Of It
- Care And Show Respect Through My Words And Actions
- Consciously Build A Legacy Starting Now, Today And Everyday
- Live A Life Of Integrity And Honour
- Make My Family, My Nation And My God Proud
- So Help Me God

I wish every Nigerian would make these set of values a part of their mentality and character in all they do. Should that happen, not only would our nation enjoy rapid developments in all aspects but also the noble achievements of any remnant leader we are blessed with will be preserved, sustained and consolidated.

2. Ndidi Okonkwo Nwuneli

Ndidi Okonkwo Nwuneli is a social reformer, with a firm belief in national development through strategic training and empowerment. In 2002, she established the Leadership, Effectiveness, Accountability & Professionalism (LEAP) organization, with the mission to inspire, empower and equip a new cadre of African leaders by providing skills and tool for personal, organizational and community transformation.

Her areas of concentration include youth development, employability, entrepreneurship, social responsibility, social innovation and SME development. She has successfully launched LEAP in 26 cities in Nigeria, with programs that are influencing and empowering thousands of Nigerians to become change agents and high performing individuals, rather than complainers and destroyers.

3. Vincent Anigbogu

Professor Vincent Anigbogu is the Director-General, Institute for National Transformation International, which has a core responsibility to develop value-based leaders who are inspired to transform their families, organizations, communities, and nations to greater levels of performance and achievements. As a passionate believer in the potentials of Africa and Nigeria, he has for some years now been spearheading advocacy for Nigeria's rebirth. However, he also believes that there cannot be true national transformation until there is a concerted effort at developing the nation's human capital.

To this end, he has been organizing conferences and initiating programs and projects aimed at orientating and installing leaders of responsibility, integrity, compassion, and excellence. His ultimate goal is to see that these leaders are strategically dispersed in seven key spheres of the Nigerian society: education, government, business, media, social (family), religious, and entertainment.

4. John Osa-Oni

Bishop John Osa-Oni is the Executive Director of Rebirth of Africa House, which was birthed with the vision to drive holistic restoration of Africa in government, economy, family, academics, religion, sports & entertainment, culture & tradition as well as media & technology - by the year 2020.

With the weapons of prolific writing, warfare prayers and intercessions, powerful prophecies, strategic projects and influential programs, he has consistently striven to awaken the consciousness of Africans and Nigerians to the fact that this century has been divinely positioned to be the "African Century". To achieve this, he has been emphasizing the need for a Kingdom-centred government through a transformed, informed, patriotic, united and positive-minded citizenry.

5. Ola Orekunrin

At a time when many young Nigerians are giving the country a bad reputation for fraud and other vices, Dr Olamide Orekunrin is making a difference and her efforts are being globally acclaimed. She is the founder of Flying Doctors Nigeria, the first air ambulance service in West Africa, transporting victims of medical emergencies, including industrial workers from the country's booming oil and gas sector.

The circumstances that led to her pioneering enterprise were such that could have many become bitter antagonists of their nation; instead she decided to do something positive about the disappointment she experienced. She was studying to become a doctor in the UK some years back when her 12-year-old younger sister who had fallen seriously ill while travelling in Nigeria, eventually died because she couldn't access the needful medical expertise urgently. The sad experience stayed with her for a long time, even after graduating as one of the youngest medical doctors in Britain – and then she decided to do something about the situation. She quit her high-flying job in the UK and decided to focus on meeting a crucial need in the Nigerian healthcare sector.

Through her air ambulance operations, hundreds of critically ill and injured people have been rapidly moved from remote areas to hospitals for urgent attention. According to her, "From patients with road traffic trauma, to bomb blast injuries to gunshot wounds, we save lives by moving these patients and providing a high level of care en route."

6. Chinelo Bob-Osamor

Chinelo is the executive producer of the Television show called Discourse. She is changing lives across Nigeria through her show and charity organization. This highly informative and educative public enlightenment program, has been transmitted on various television stations for over 10 years. She started with a show called Healthwise in the year 2000. Healthwise won an award from the Association of Resident Doctors. The award-winning program was the only health program on television in Abuja for a long time. Both television programs were created by Chinelo Bob-Osamor. Healthwise was the precursor of Discourse and it featured medical consultants in varied fields of medicine discussing topical diseases and health related issues.

Building on the popularity of Healthwise and a deluge of request from the public to reach out and discuss issues other than health, she produced Discourse in 2004. The program focuses on how the activities of government, government agencies, organized private sector and individuals impact society. Health issues are also given pride of place in Discourse.

After many years of successful broadcast to audiences in Abuja and Lagos, Bob-Osamor is set to expand the benefits of the program to a wider audience in other states of the federation through a collaboration with particular state television stations. She hopes this will afford majority of Nigerians access to the rich content of the program which focuses on their health and other major issues that plague the nation. The program is already in six states and Abuja and hopes to take on two additional states each quarter till most of the states of the federation are covered.

Chinelo Bob-Osamor, the executive producer of Discourse holds a Bachelor of Science Degree (B.sc) in political science and an LLB Degree from Universities of Jos and Lagos respectively. She was called to the Nigerian Bar in 1996. She is also the Chairman Board of Trustees of Chike Okagbue Foundation (COF), an educational and philanthropic foundation which she established to honor the memory of her late father Chike Okagbue. The foundation currently has 60 students on full scholarship in various secondary schools.

7. Christopher Okoh

Christopher Onyekachukwu Okoh is one of the vibrant Nigerians demonstrating the truth that no one is too young or too isolated to make meaningful contributions to national development.

A long-term advocate of impactful living, he seized the opportunity of the National Youth Service Corps program in 2010 to volunteer to be a Development Knowledge Facilitator (DKF) with emphasis on the Millennium Development Goals (MDGs) in Nigeria. He devoted his time in his place of posting in Anambra State to humanitarian services, through knowledge sharing and value re-orientation. He took his campaigns to educational institutions, streets, health centers, markets and everywhere within his state of national service.

Within the brief service year, he initiated skills acquisition programs, as well as sensitization activities on issues of personal hygiene, HIV/AIDS and environmental education. He also donated writing materials, brooms and wastebaskets to primary and secondary schools. At the end of his service year the state's Commissioner honoured him with a commendation certificate for excellent performance for Youths and Sports. He was also conferred with a certificate of merit on outstanding implementation of MDGs.

8. Funmi Iyanda

Olufunmilola Aduke Iyanda's story also serves to show that anyone, from any walk of life, could choose to make a difference. She was a professional broadcaster, who produced and hosted Nigeria's popular and authoritative talk show, New Dawn with Funmi. It was while doing the show in 2002 that the medical case of a young child with a hole in his heart was brought to her attention. A huge sum of money was needed to treat him but his parents could not afford it. Funmi had to use her program to appeal for fund to help the child. Even though the child eventually died, the money that was raised helped to save two other young children.

Touched by what she experienced while trying to save these children, she soon founded Change-A-Life (CAL) foundation, a social service non-profit organization which functions as an education and health support scheme for gifted but underprivileged children who have lost a parent or both. The organization also assists the parents and guardians of its educational beneficiaries by awarding grants for them to start or maintain their businesses. Since inception, the foundation has helped save many lives and enhanced capacity building. Its primary avenues for rendering support include: educational scholarships, business grants, young adult mentoring, adult and community education, women empowerment, and civic engagement.

9. Grace Ihejiamaizu

Grace is one of the young Nigerian entrepreneurs and change agents privately driving transformation through information, re-orientation and capacity building. Still in her 20s, she is the founder and executive director of iKapture Networks (formerly known as RYPE Initiative), an afterschool youth development organization strategically focused on providing education and leadership services to secondary and post-secondary students in Nigeria using creative learning methods and ICT. She is also the founder and chief editor of Opportunity Desk, one of the largest online platforms for global opportunities with over 100,000 visits monthly. Through her initiatives, hundreds of young people have been trained, engaged and empowered to live productive and successful lives.

10. Sani Bello

Col. Sani Bello (rtd) is the founder of the Sani Bello Foundation, which has the laudable vision of targeting, enlightening and empowering young minds from northern Nigerian who have often been exploited for criminal and troublemaking activities. What the foundation does is evacuation and rehabilitation of unemployed, homeless youths and street urchins to a well-organized environment and structure where they are trained in diverse entrepreneurial skills. Its pilot states are Niger, Kaduna and Kano.

To achieve its desired goal of youth empowerment through entrepreneurship, the foundation offers training on catering and hospitality, fashion design, farm management, computer maintenance technology and GSM repair.

Each of these illustrious minds that I have highlighted here, as well as many others like them, has a message and challenge for every Nigerian. No one is too small, too big or too young to contribute to the rebirth of Nigeria. The desire of every one of them is that we all join hands as concerned citizens to rebuild Nigeria in our own little ways. As one of them (Sani Bello) once said:

> **"The time has passed when we have to wait for Government to do everything for us; it's now time private individuals got involved in mobilizing support activities that will move the nation forward."**

It is my belief that initiatives like these ones we have seen above must be in their millions in a large country like ours. I am convinced that it is time for the citizens to stop looking up to the government to do all these alone. Let's take up the challenge to ourselves; let's begin to build our own country as we can. It is our country - we should not wait for anyone to build it for us.

For the sake of my beloved country I have decided to relocate from Europe where I have lived the last 30 years of my life and move back to Nigeria, to join the efforts of my people to create a better future and destiny for all people of Nigeria and Africa. It is my plan to do something for every State. I wish to establish something concrete and tangible that will improve the lives of Nigerians all over the nation.

I am not talking about just church or religious outreaches. My primary concern right now is to bring improvement to the living standard and well-being of Nigerians so that they could in turn go and lift up the hands of their fellow African brethren.

I pray and hope to come back to Nigeria with a large group of Europeans and peoples of other nationalities for whom I have lived and served the last 30 years, so that they too might help to alleviate the suffering of my people.

GOLDEN TRUTHS
FROM CHAPTER 8

- We must go beyond complaining and daydreaming to individually contribute to building a New Nigeria.

- Rebuilding Nigeria is primarily in the hands of the Nigerian citizens and not the government.

- Every Nigerian has a role to play; none is too unfit to contribute.

- Many Nigerians have realized these truths and have embarked on individual initiatives that are transforming the nation, but they need the support of all other Nigerians who will equally imbibe good and helpful value systems.

Part Three

GOVERNANCE RE-EVALUATION AND VALUE RE-ORIENTATION

9

IS DEMOCRACY A VIABLE OPTION FOR NIGERIA?

It has been said that democracy is the worst form of government except all the others that have been tried.

—Winston Churchill

It was not surprising that when the Nigerian state assumed a new governance status in 1999 following the end of military regime in the country it was greeted with national celebration. Military dictatorship, which had fast-tracked the crippling of the nation, was replaced by representative democracy with the hopes and aspirations of good governance much higher than what it had been in previous years.

Now, after a hundred years of its existence as a nation, and after fifty-five years of political independence and self-rule, and in spite of all the challenges it has faced and still faces, there is no doubt that Nigeria has come a long way in its evolution as a nation and in its various attempts to institutionalize a system of government in the country.

As the nation marked 16 years of uninterrupted democratic rule on May 29, 2015, analysts agreed that the journey from independence to this point had been a long roller-coaster of anticipation, disillusionment, skepticism and hope.

Incidentally, the country, at various times in its chequered history, has had different systems of government foisted on it: from monarchical rule to military regimes to democratic system of government. Unfortunately, none of these seems to have been able to add much value to the citizens or extricate the country from the manacles of neo-colonialism.

With regards to democratic governance especially, as I have repeatedly noted so far, there is a deep feeling of disenchantment among the masses after having expected so much and only got so little. It is this worrying state that has left many wondering if democracy is actually the most suitable system of government for the country.

POSSIBLE ALTERNATIVES?

But let us assume for a moment that we do away with democracy. What alternatives do we have? A few suggestions have been made, and I will attempt here to briefly look at three of them. One of the suggested alternatives is the Chinese state capitalism, led by the communist party. Looking at the boom that the Chinese economy has apparently experienced in recent years, as well as the relatively socio-political stability the country enjoys, many have suggested that their system of government is exactly what Nigeria needs. But how true is this, really?

> **Personally, I consider it laughable to even imagine that communism is a desirable form of government, not to talk of recommending it for Nigeria.**

The truth is that despite the façade of economic progress and political stability, communist countries are autocratic by default. Who wants to be led by a government where the Head of State can easily exploit the concentration of power in the centre and turn himself into a sadistic dictator, paranoid of criticism, mauling perceived enemies of the government and constantly seeking to control every aspect of the citizens' lives?

Who wants to be under a government where the rule of law means little or nothing; where respect for basic human rights is dependent on the mood or whim of the leader? I don't see how this can augur well for Nigeria in any way. That aside, what many do not know about the Chinese society is that it is not a pure free-market economy because the economy is still vastly influenced by political policy, which is different from what obtains in a democratic system.

However, the Chinese political structure aside, there is a more dominant alternative being proffered by some segments of the Nigerian society. This alternative is military rule. Proponents of this idea are of the view that Nigerians have largely become used to the culture of corruption, indiscipline, self-centredness and impatience, and thus need an iron hand to rule them. It is largely believed that, since the military institution is the exact opposite of indiscipline, only a military government can reorientate Nigerians and awaken their consciousness to their roles in nation building.

This assumption is further corroborated by the fact that

observations have shown that citizens quickly behave themselves anytime and anywhere they find military men. Consequently, it is believed that the military will do a better job in making Nigerians obedient to law and order. But again, we must ask, how true is this? Will the military actually do a better job than a democratic government?

Let me clearly state again that, as in the case of communism, militarism as a system of government cannot be said to be suitable for Nigeria in whatever form or guise. This is because in military regimes, as Nigeria has experienced for many years, the army is always used to subvert and suppress the people's wishes and desires. Military administrators are accountable to no one since they are neither elected nor appointed by the people. They do not really care about the people; so they just go ahead and do what they want to do in whatever way they deem fit, even if they have to abuse the fundamental human rights of the citizens.

As for the argument on militarised reorientation and fostering of discipline among the populace, I think this should sound really worrisome and demeaning to us. Rather than accepting it as a reason to accept and glorify military rule, it should rather give us serious concern. Why do we need to see guns, uniforms and brutality before we imbibe the right value systems? Why do we have to wait till we are bullied and beaten before we have to behave decently? Are we saying we have not developed to the point thinking for ourselves and knowing what is right? Are we saying Nigerians are so slow in thinking to the point that they need military batons and battalions before conducting ourselves as rational human beings?

In other words, are we simply comparing ourselves with animals that have to be domesticated, trained and guided to know what should be done? Are we indirectly validating the twisted thinking of the masterminds of the slave trade who claimed their actions was based on the fact that we were not much different from baboons because of our level of reasoning? No, this should not be.

Self-degradation aside, I believe the majority of Nigerians can still remember the dark days of military autocracy when men in uniform trampled upon the civic rights and individual liberties of the people with flagrant impunity. They still remember how many innocent Nigerians were thrown into prison without trial or after a kangaroo trial. They still remember the violent suppression of any form of organized civil disobedience, the bloodletting and senseless killings of many Nigerians, their only crime being that they dared to challenge the tyranny and intolerance of military dictators controlling the affairs of the nation, and demand that citizens' rights be respected.

Many Nigerians can still vividly remember how their collective wealth was brazenly stolen under military rule without any restriction. Evidently therefore, because Nigerians remember, I'm sure we no longer want to travel that road; we no longer want to return to this dark period of our history. Do we? Certainly not! We must move on for good.

Then there is another group of people who are suggesting a fusion of the military rule with democratic government, or simply milidemocracy. According to one of the proponents, milidemocracy involves "meshing what is good about the military, i.e. decisiveness, tolerance and discipline; and what is great about civilians, i.e. inclusiveness and locality. Together, both institutions can forge a system that works well and work best for the country and still achieve the basic aims of western democracy: accountability and responsiveness in an atmosphere of constitutionalism."

On how this should be implemented, the same proponent said, "This, the new Nigerian constitution must do. The military and civilian institutions should band together to make this a viable reality. There is no need to exclude the military from government. As a matter of urgency therefore, we need to set up agencies to map out the structures and modalities for such a new thinking."

Let me state clearly that while this form of government may seem like the perfect proposition in the imagination of some people, in reality however, it is at best impracticable and at worst ridiculous. Military rule and democratic government are two mutually exclusive concepts because they share conflicting tenets. Their modes of assuming power, the institutions through which they administer control and their attitudes to the constitution of the country are in absolute contrast.

Military rule is government by the armed forces who often seize power without the consent of the people, as opposed to what obtains in a democracy. And since I have already expressed disagreement on the suggestion of military involvement in governance, I wouldn't want to dwell much on the incongruity of milidemocracy or any such concept.

The point I'm trying to make here is that regardless of what may have happened so far, I still strongly believe that democracy remains the best form of government for Nigeria and any nation on earth for that matter. While it is true that democracy has suffered many contradictions, especially in African countries and Nigerians in particular, we must not lose sight of the greater good - the enormous advantages that democracy has over other systems of governance. Neither should we forget or ignore the very important fact.

> **The seeming ineffectiveness of democracy in Nigeria is not because the concept in itself is defective or impractical but simply because the majority of Nigerians themselves are either ignorant of its meaning or refusing to comply with its tenets.**

At this juncture, I must attempt a clarification of the concept.

DEFINING DEMOCRACY

Democracy is best described as a system of government in which the power to rule resides with the people through their elected representatives.

The term democracy is derived from the Greek word "dēmokratiā", which is the derivative of the combination of the words "demos" which means "people", and "kratos" which implies "rule" or "authority". It was coined in the middle of the 5th century BC to mean the political system of rule that existed then in some Greek city-states, notably Athens. This therefore means that democracy is rule or authority by the people.

Ex-American president, Abraham Lincoln, in his Gettysburg address, gave what has perhaps become the most popular definition of democracy. According to him, democracy is the "government of the people, by the people, and for the people."

This definition again emphasises that the people are both the subject and object of democracy. To me therefore, this means that democracy is all about the people. As a system of government, it recognizes and emphasizes the rights of the citizens, and the role they have to play in the way and manner they are governed.

As I already emphasized, irrespective of the current political, social and economic challenges in the country, I believe that democracy remains the best system of government for us as a nation.

One of the foremost advantages that democracy has over other forms of government is effective participation - the opportunity for the citizenry to participate in the process of the selection and election of their leaders and representatives. We, the people, are able to participate in governance; it gives us the opportunity of participating in the political process, and in decision-making, thereby disallowing any form of aristocracy or authoritarianism.

Democracy has as one of its core principles the recognition of the sovereignty of the people, since the government in the first place is for them. The feeling of inclusiveness, where each and every member of the 'people' is entitled to participate in governance brings about a feeling of satisfaction and a sense patriotism that is necessary for the development of a heterogeneous state such as Nigeria.

Unlike other forms of government where priority is not placed on the people, the citizens have the opportunity to have their say on any matter or policy affecting them and to make their voices heard. Moreover, the people have the right to vote and be voted for. They have the ability to decide who governs them, and also reject whoever is not representing them properly.

More so, only in democracy is the freedom of speech exclusively guaranteed. Since this is one of the basic tenets of democracy, the voice of the people is respected and the citizens are allowed to have their say without any form of inhibition. Other fundamental human rights, such as the freedom of religion, right to life, right to own property, freedom of association, are also respected in a democratic setting.

In addition, I like to say that democracy is also a system of equality. An ideal feature of ideal democracy is that each and every member of the citizenry is equal before the law. This equality cuts across every responsibility and privilege afforded the people by the state. What this means, therefore, is that every citizen has equal right to vote and have his vote counted equally with the votes of others; equal right to request, gather and disseminate information as any other member of the state; equal right to participate on an equal footing with other members of the citizenry in the exercise of control of the policy or agenda of the country. It is a universal reality that no other form of government can guarantee these.

Although I do know that there are some who may want to argue that even during democratic dispensations, as being currently practiced in Nigeria, the rights and freedoms of citizens are sometimes subtly curtailed and undermined by the government through the security agencies. An example of this was the alleged ban by the police on public rallies organized by some Nigerians demanding the release of the abducted Chibok girls. There was also the shameful clampdown on the media, when the distribution vans of some newspaper houses where stopped, searched, and some copies of the day's paper were seized by the military under the ridiculous excuse of searching for arms belonging to the radical Islamic sect, Boko Haram.

However, let me state clearly that this can only happen in an abnormal democratic setting and not in the ideal. Democracy in Nigeria at present is still at its infantile stage, even after 15 years. It is still growing and therefore, should not become the standard yardstick for measuring true democracy. Having said that, it is also pertinent for me to state that even when the government has committed such human rights violations, the voices of the people had prevailed, not suppressed, and the government had backpedalled. This can only happen in a democracy.

Very importantly, democracy creates informed electorates or citizenry. As a result of the fact that members of the public have the opportunity to know about and participate in national issues, they are able to learn about existing policies and their alternatives – as well as their likely consequences. This way, citizens are more enlightened and actively involved in matters of the state.

In addition, let me state here that democracy brings a country to the focus of the world, and into the map of international honor and glory. It brings respect to a country in the committee of nations. These have been achieved by countries such as Great Britain and the United States of America known as the home of democracy. Nigeria also can be part of this League of Nations.

IS DEMOCRACY REALLY FOREIGN TO NIGERIA?

There are those who believe that the reason why democracy in Nigeria and in many parts of Africa has suffered tremendous setbacks is because it was a system of government foisted on us by the western world and that it didn't evolve from the people themselves. Therefore, the concept had no root or basis in the traditional Nigerian or African indigenous political culture. The argument is that traditional African societies practiced a monarchical system of government and therefore, we should have continued with this system rather than importing another form from the West.

Monarchy is a form of government in which a state or region is governed by an individual who inherited the throne by birth, or by being the most qualified by virtue of royalty. Such an individual usually rules for life or until he abdicates the position of authority by whatever means. In other words, sovereignty is vested in the individual who is the monarch.

While it is true that many traditional Nigerian communities practiced a monarchical system of government before the coming of the Europeans, it could also be argued that even the monarchical system of government as practiced by some ancient African societies share some similarities with democracy.

For example, the old Oyo Empire practiced a strong and undisputable form of 'traditional democracy'. There existed in the old Oyo empire, an inviolable democratic principle of separation of powers, which is aimed at making sure that whoever the chief executive was did not arrogate too much power to himself and his cronies.

According to Adeyinka and Ojo (2014), any Alaafin in the old Oyo Empire who attempted to arrogate to himself extra constitutional powers did so to his peril as he would be asked to 'sleep' (die by committing suicide) by the Basorun. According to them, the very fact that chiefs existed in the corridor of power to advise and assist the "Yoruba sovereign provided a counterweight against monarchical absolutism."

When an offending Alaafin was rejected, one of the pronouncements the Basorun (a sort of prime minister and commander-in-chief of the armed forces) made was "...the people reject you". This according to them is in perfect agreement with the submission of Casely Hayford (1913) that "The office of the king is elective. No king, that is to say, is born a king... It is the right of those who placed him there to put him off the stool for any just cause. But no other authority can rightly interfere with his position, if his people are satisfied with him."

More so, Adeyinka and Ojo went on to give another instance of the Benin Empire where the Benin people because of the perceived highhandedness of the Ogiso kings rejected the Ogiso Dynasty. Does this not correspond with what democracy is all about? Where the people decide who leads them and also reserve the power to remove any unpopular, selfish and dictatorial leader? Is it not therefore misplaced to assume that the reason democracy has suffered constant breakdown in Nigeria is because it had no root or foundation in the indigenous political culture of the people?

From the foregoing therefore, it is clear that the indigenous system of government practiced by traditional Nigerian societies possessed some similarities with modern democracy in which those who hold political positions are regarded as representatives of the people and trustees of the people's trust. It is such that has established forms of checks and balances, which restrain the exercise of disproportionate or excessive display of power by those who wield it, and also provides appropriate punishments or sanctions for any perceived abuse and misuse of political power.

ARE OTHER FORMS OF POWER STRUCTURE BETTER?

As we continue in this discussion, let me quickly look at another assumption of some other people. There are those who believe that democracy is too expensive. Their argument is that organizing nationwide elections, conducting public hearings, and then having three tiers of government and other paraphernalia of democracy amount to a needless waste of unavailable resources and time. Thus, they propose that other forms, such as aristocracy are better because resources will be conserved and utilized better. In their minds, everybody does not need to be involved in government; it should be left for the few privileged elites. By the way, aristocracy is a system of government in which a few elites bear rule over the majority of the people.

> **Do we really agree with this school of thought? Should we leave the governance of our nation, the administration of our collective destiny, in the hands of a privileged few? I beg to disagree.**

With the wind of democracy blowing across the world, other forms of government like communism, authoritarianism, totalitarianism, militarism or aristocracy have become outdated and needless. I make bold to say this.

If it is then so good, what is the problem with democracy in Nigeria? Why has it not added much value to the lives of the people? Why is it that instead of benefiting the majority of the people (since that is the aim) it has only helped to widen the chasm between the rich and the poor; between the leaders and the led?

The truth, as I said before, is that the problem is not with democracy as a concept or as a system of government but with the way it is practiced in the Nigeria. Most Nigerians are abdicating their power and responsibilities to their leaders. But that is not what democracy is all about. Democracy is all about the power of the people, for the people and by the people.

In a democracy it is the people that take responsibility for their actions. They take responsibility for the growth and development of their nation. They take responsibility for their economy. They take responsibility for their advancement and civilization. Even though there is a place for leadership, but leadership only stops in the area of giving direction and casting vision.

The key point here is that democracy on its own, does not guarantee good governance. It does not necessarily translate into automatic development and improvement of the nation. At least the Nigerian experience can prove that. Democracy is not an end in itself but a means to an end; it is a means by which we can attain and achieve all the things we hope to see in our nation.

Democracy truly is a vehicle for a country's emancipation from stagnancy and deprivation. However, it is we, the people, who must be the drivers of the development we seek by embracing right attitudes and values. It is we who must put machineries in place to make democracy get us to where we want to go. This is the distinct platform democracy affords us; to take our destiny in our hands and protect our welfare as a people.

For true democracy to be achieved and sustained in Nigeria then, all hands must be on deck to make it work. Consequently, as we practice democracy, it behooves us, the demos, to imbibe noble values, demand good governance, and show respect for the rule of law.

> **We must insist upon good governance that ensures improved welfare of the people, reduction in the cost of governance, accountability and transparency in the conduct of the affairs of the country and the eradication of corruption.**

Furthermore, we must also insist on the independence of the judiciary, which is regarded as the last hope of the common man. Only by ensuring that these are put in place can we actually say we are practicing a true democracy. Then, and only then, can we actually move our nation towards upward political and socio-economic advancement.

Now, despite all the points I have made above in favor of democracy, I cannot but state my belief that democracy in itself is not a perfect system, especially when it comes to Africa. Even in America, which is the cradle of modern democracy, the Founding Fathers realized the defects and weaknesses of democracy. Hence they built a system around it to curb and guard against its weaknesses.

Have you ever heard of the Electoral College? That is a safeguard system to deal with the deficiencies of democracy. Have you also heard of conversations whereby the person who got the most popular votes in a general election in America never actually became the president as in the case of the presidential election between Al Gore/George Bush? Do you know why that happens? Simply put, it is because despite the fact that those people got the popular vote, they never got the Electoral College vote which is a complex system that is not the topic of discussion here.

In the case of Bush/Gore, George W. Bush was declared the winner of the election and became the 43rd president of the United States of America but he never got the most votes. He did not win the presidential election by popular vote. Al Gore gathered 540,000 more votes than Bush; however Bush was declared the winner of the election and became the president.

In 1888, Benjamin Harrison became the president of America despite the fact that he had 90,000 less votes than Grover Cleveland. This same thing happened in the election of 1876 and 1824 when those who had the most votes never won the presidency.

I personally see the ingenuity and foresight in the Founding Father's wisdom by creating the Electoral College system. The basic idea of an electoral college is that some individuals carry more weight with their voter's cards than others; these are called electors. In the same vein some states carry more weight than others. That means individuals are rated by their status and standing as registered by electoral colleges. Therefore, at the end of the day, up till now in the United States of America, we have states where their votes carry more weight than other states. Also there are some individuals whose votes carry more weight than other individuals. This actually seems like a contradiction to the tenets of democracy.

So, why do I agree with this principle? It must be remembered that at the time of America's independence, when democracy was being established, a large number of the populace were not educated. It would therefore be an exercise in self-deception if they just blindly said that they had democracy and everybody's vote was equal, no matter who they were (e.g., a homeless loafer and an attorney general).

It is judging from that belief (that some people understand the political process better than other citizens that are not even educated) that gave birth to the idea of Electoral College where citizens who already have some amount of weight, influence and clout in the society are registered to vote as having special privileges attached to them. The amount of votes that is credited to you depends on your status in the society.

I am not advocating that we should do exactly the same thing in Nigeria, but a similar system is definitely needed. Especially in a country where we have about 50 percent of the population of our country as illiterate. Some of the citizens don't even understand what a party's political program is all about. It is therefore no wonder why it is rather easy for corrupt politicians to buy their way through this usually gullible group of electorates.

So, if somebody is illiterate and doesn't even know the names of the candidate, the party's manifesto, the values of the country and we count the vote of such an individual as equal to that of a senior advocate of Nigeria who can analyze and give logical conclusions, then we are just playing democracy. I personally believe that there is wisdom in using people's value systems and track records to determine their significance in a voting process. So, my submission is that democracy must be practiced in Nigeria and indeed in the whole of Africa with some African peculiarities.

Unfortunately for Africa, and may I say for most parts of the world, when the American government propagates and exports (if not impose) democracy on other countries, they don't mention what the Founding Fathers did and they don't usually say anything about the Electoral College. Very few individuals, even in America, know what the Electoral College is, much less outside of America, where we try to copy America's model of democracy.

I hope to be able to deliberate further in a future book about the form of democratic system that is eligible for the African continent. Here, however, I simply want to tell my fellow Nigerians and Africans not to blindly follow the dictates of the so called western nations. I am concerned that African nations are easily manipulated and indeed frightened by the calls for democracy. It is almost a cuss word to an African leader to say he is not democratic. So, in our quest to be seemingly democratic, we swallow the pill and automatically do two four-year terms, as if this is the standard for democracy. So if you want to even suggest that a leader in Africa stays for more than two terms you are immediately assumed to be advocating for dictatorship.

My take is that two four-year terms governance might not be ideal for the African situation as for most developing countries. The reason is because of what I had mentioned in a previous chapter in this book. Whenever an African country is fortunate enough to come across a remnant leader as in the case of Awolowo, Murtala, Obasanjo, Buhari/Idiagbon governments, it is more or less wise to allow them stay, even if it means altering the constitution to do that. Since these are people with above average performance in comparison with other African leaders, their prolonged stay will promote stability and prosperity, as well as establish institutions that will bring about accelerated progress in national development.

As I said previously, I have to write a different book about this topic because there are many factors that must be looked into before this can be considered. We have to make sure that there is a strong and viable legislature system that cannot be controlled by the executive. In short, measures must be put in place to prevent the country from slipping into autocracy and dictatorship.

Right now, I am following a similar debate in some countries of Africa as I am writing this book. Even though Rwanda and Burundi are neighboring countries, I would gladly support an extension of stay in power for the Rwandan president, Paul Kagame, while I will oppose a prolonged stay in power for the president of Burundi, Pierre Nkurunziza. The reason for this is because of the track records of these incumbents. In my personal opinion, Paul Kagame's record shows that he deserves to stay in power for a longer period, while Pierre Nkurunziza's record doesn't give me that same assurance.

> **What I am trying to say is that democracy must be practiced considering the peculiar situation of the African continent. A continent where majority of the people don't have a clue into the intricacies of politics; a continent where we have had such bad record of leadership.**

It is therefore in my opinion rather naïve or foolish of us if when we find one godly leader we let him lead for just eight years, simply because we want to please the so called western countries who tell us that democracy means two four-year terms for an elective office.

The stand of the western countries about lack of democracy in Africa only serves to confirm their hypocrisy. In their nations, when the need calls for it, they amend the constitution - as in the case of Franklin D. Roosevelt who was elected into office for four terms. He could have served all the four terms if not that he died in office soon after winning the fourth election. America was going through the Great Depression and the Second World War at that time and they needed a strong leader to steer the ship of the nation to safety.

Most people would not believe that in Great Britain they don't have two-term limit for their Prime Ministers. For instance, Sir Robert Walpole, regarded as the first Prime Minister of Britain, was in office for 20 years. More recently, Margaret Thatcher ruled for 11 years, and Tony Blair was in office for 10 years. Imagine that. A British Prime Minister ruled for 20 years and no one is calling that dictatorship.

The same thing happens in France. Some of their Prime Ministers led the country for more than a decade. Francois Mitterrand was in office for 14 years, and Charles De Gaulle was in office for a decade, and nobody cried foul.

In Germany, some of their Chancellors ruled for more than a decade in office and no one calls them dictators. Konrad Adenauer ruled for 14 years and Helmut Kohl ruled for 16 years.

Spain, under the rule of Francisco Franco, was a total dictatorship in today's terms, but he brought the country out of poverty into prosperity. He was in office for 39 years. Another Prime Minster of Spain, Felipe Gonzalez, was in office for 14 years.

Lee Kwan Yew that is so much celebrated in Africa would have been termed a diehard dictator if he was an African because he ruled Singapore for more than 3 decades, but he brought his country from the third world to first world in one generation.

China would also be called a dictatorship, but the likes of Mao Zedong who ruled for 27 years, Deng Xiaoping, who ruled for 11 years, among many others, were able to make their country become one of the biggest economies in the world today. Even Hong Kong that is still being controlled by China is not a complete democracy by western standards, but because of the progress it boasts of, no one is calling it a dictatorship.

Please let me remind you that I am not for dictatorship but I just want to point out that whenever we have remnant leaders who are exceptionally gifted with the right value systems, we should consider giving them an opportunity to bring about a total transformation in our nations. Of course this should only be after considering all factors that will help mitigate against any form of dictatorship or perpetual rule by one man.

Even today it is hard to call Russian government a democracy with Vladimir Putin; but it cannot be denied that he is restoring the prosperity and dignity of the nation. Other nations like Malaysia, Saudi Arabia, Kuwait, United Arab Emirates and a large part of the Middle Eastern countries don't even practice democracy in any form, yet the western democracy is silent about them because the interest of the west is there; but when it comes to Africa we are bullied into submission.

I am absolutely certain that if President Olusegun Obasanjo had been allowed to remain for a third term in office, the country would have avoided most of the woes it is going through right now. There would not have been the sordid stories with Umar Yar'Adua and the tragedies of corruption in Goodluck Jonathan's administration.

While many may perceive me as a proponent of dictatorship because of this viewpoint of mine, let me emphasize it again that I am just trying to be realistic about the reality on ground in Nigeria and other African countries. We need to practice the best model of democracy for us, not the pattern prescribed by someone else.

As I have said above, this is a topic for another book, but I am glad this topic has been opened for discussion. We have to see how to make democracy more palatable for the country of Nigeria and the continent of Africa.

In the case of the western nations where the pot is already cleansed, it is easier to choose any candidate and he will perform. In our own case however, where our value system is largely compromised, it is going to be a challenge for some time for us not to keep repeating the mistakes of getting corrupt leaders to replace the good remnant leaders. To avoid that, it might just be a great idea to allow those remnant leaders to hang on for as long as the people want them.

Again, as I conclude this chapter, I maintain that whatever the case may be, democracy is the best system of government the world has seen; yet it could be modified to serve us better. We have to admit that democracy is the dictatorship of the majority - that is, a dictatorship of the majority that took the vote but not necessarily the dictatorship of the best. Nigeria, like no other country, can testify to this after the 16 years of PDP-led government. Yes, the PDP was a majority party, in fact, the largest in Africa at one time; but that does not necessarily mean the rule of the best. It is in my quest to find answers to such a dilemma that I have decided to include this chapter.

GOLDEN TRUTHS
FROM CHAPTER 9

- Due to perceived ineffectiveness of democracy in Nigeria, there have been alternative suggestions, including communism, militarism and milidemocracy.

- Communism is undesirable for Nigeria because it is autocratic by default.

- Suggestion of continued military rule is degrading, as it portrays Nigerians as people who behave decently only when they see guns, uniforms and brutality.

- Milidemocracy is impracticable because military rule and democractic government are two mutually exclusive concepts.

- Democracy is still the best form of government for Nigeria. The reason democracy seems unsuitable for Nigeria is because of ignorance of its meaning, and non-compliance to its tenets.

- Democracy is not entirely new to Nigeria, as some pre-colonial traditional systems of government had features of democracy.

- Democracy is not an end in itself; all hands – from the citizens to the leaders – must be on deck to make it work.

- Democracy in Africa must be adapted to the peculiarities of the continent.

10

STRONG MEN OR STRONG INSTITUTIONS?

"In the 21st century, capable, reliable, and transparent institutions are the key to success: strong parliaments, honest police forces, independent judges, an independent press, a vibrant private sector, a civil society. Those are the things that give life to democracy, because that is what matters in people's everyday lives... Africa doesn't need strong men, it needs strong institutions."

—President Barack Obama

The issue raised in the above statement by the current President of the United States to the Ghanaian Parliament on July 11, 2009 can be seen as constituting the heart of the maladies depriving Nigeria of fully enjoying the dividends of democracy and joining the ranks of developed nations. In fact, it was as if President Obama was indirectly addressing Nigeria and Nigerians, though physically present in Ghana.

Building formidable institutions has been a difficult task for post-Independence Nigeria. Obviously, Nigeria has all it takes to be a strong, viable and productive nation in all spheres, but for the prioritisation of strong men over strong institutions. In other words, we are where we are today as a nation because we have so many powerful men dominating our national lives where powerful institutions ought to have been put in place.

Nothing disturbs a nation's internal stability and sense of wellbeing more profoundly than the absence of workable, effective and efficient institutions. Daniel Chirot, Professor of International Studies at the University of Washington, explicitly expressed that, "underdevelopment of a country is the result of its deficient value system and economic structures".

Chirot's observation clearly supports the idea that good value systems and strong institutions or structures are the bedrock of effectiveness, progress, and socio-economic and political balance in any society. It therefore implies that no society can develop beyond the level of the workable institutions it has put in place.

DEMYSTIFYING THE CONCEPTS

For the sake of clarity, let me state that the term "strong men" usually refers to influential persons who wield enormous power and charisma and thus can easily dictate to institutions and people what they should do. They are dominant movers and shakers who have both the clout and the resources to enforce their wishes and demands.

> **Especially within the Nigeria context, strong men have come to mean the untouchable juggernauts, the hallowed godfathers and the "sacred cows" who see themselves as a special breed of people to whom the country owes special allegiance.**

National institutions on the other hand, describe institutions established by law to carry out certain functions with the ultimate aim of safeguarding the sovereignty, security, and stability of a nation, as well as fostering the general development, progress and well-being of the citizens. These institutions therefore are said to be strong when they operate adequately and take decisions independently, based on the laws or codes establishing them without external interference from any source.

By this, I mean that strong institutions are those which independently perform their statutory functions according to laid down laws, without any external influence, coercion or direction. Nigeria's national institutions include the Judiciary, the Nigeria Police Force, the Independent Corrupt Practices and other related crimes Commission (ICPC), Nigeria Customs Service, the Armed Forces, the Independent National Electoral Commission (INEC), the Economic and Financial Crimes Commission (EFCC), to mention a few.

PARADOX OF STRONG MEN IN NIGERIA

It is really sad to note that in our quest to get "almighty" leaders over the years, we have inadvertently done more and spent more to build strong men, without thinking of building strong institutions; nor did we think of the potential consequences of our actions and inactions. Unfortunately, these strong men have risen to a height greater than the institutions and have become cabals that hinder the progress of the nation.

These strong men have become stronger than the national institutions as they have these institutions at their mercy. Thus, as I mentioned before, the term "strong men" in Nigeria has become synonymous with men who can almost do anything without being questioned. These are men who embezzle billions of naira belonging to the citizens without anyone raising an eyebrow. These are men who can shut down the judiciary, lock up the law courts and pocket the keys with no one daring to challenge them. These, I say, are men who, at their command, soldiers can invade a community, massacre the people living there, and everybody looks the other way. These are men who will fail to appear before a legally constituted commission of enquiry, ridicule it, and thereafter be elected governor or president.

Suffice it to say that, in as much as every nation needs strong men to move forward, strong institutions are better catalysts of national progress and development. No nation can develop to its full potentials without strong and viable institutions. It therefore means that social change, economic buoyancy and opulence will continuously elude us, if we leave the affairs of nation building in the hands of a selected few.

It was for this reason that while many Nigerians were clamouring for the then APC presidential candidate (now President of the country) Muhammadu Buhari and hailing him as the "messiah" to come, a perceptive columnist, Okey Ndibe, issued this remarkable caveat on February 19, 2015:

A lot of Nigerians want Mr. Buhari to win the presidential election so that he'd handle the morass of corruption for them. Bad news alert: not going to happen! Mr. Buhari may have all the Olympian intention to wage war against corruption, but he won't go far…Corruption is a systemic plague, and it is best fought, not by one heroic individual, but through institutions. A culture that abhors corruption is key. Such abhorrence then tailors institutional tools that identify and prosecute acts of corruption, regardless of the name, religion and state of the perpetrator… The cry should not be PDP or APC, nor is the answer Jonathan or Buhari. It is, "Let us create, this day, formidable, enduring institutions that can outlive mortals strong and weak."

It is quite true that over the years, Nigeria has suffered diverse predicaments as a result of preferring strong men to strong structures and this undoubtedly can be assumed as the reason why things have constantly fallen apart in virtually every sector of our national life. In time past and even now, we have had situations where institutions, which are supposed to enhance the quality of life of the masses in the country, are manipulated to satisfy the parochial greed of a selected few. More so, it is no longer news that many strong men who partook in stifling the nation's economic growth and plunged the nation into its gloomy state have now become opinion leaders. Is this not an irony?

Most recently, we have had cases of strong men embezzling public funds amounting to millions and billions of naira to swell their foreign banks and invest abroad but we never heard of any punishment meted out to them. This is not far from the fact that they have 'long legs' or they are in the good books of the government of the day. We have had cases where incompetent and unprepared men were imposed or appointed in positions of authority, not because of their qualifications but because they are protégées of some strong men. We have had instances where court judgments were perverted and delivered in favour of someone at the top.

Such putrid system of things can only happen in a country without functional and strong national institutions. This is bad for nation building as it has set us back considerably. What Nigeria needs at the moment are strong institutions not strong men.

> **Observably, in the 21st century, nations which have attained greatness and great feats are nations which have developed dependable, workable, and transparent institutions in all facets of their national life.**

In most of the advanced countries of the world today, I cannot say they really have strong leaders. No, they no longer look for or depend on finding extraordinary leaders that will lead them to paradise. They have managed to build strong and reliable systems that function automatically, irrespective of whom the leader is, strong or weak. These are nations that have managed to build strong institutions, honest and devoted security agents, transparent judicial processes, press freedom, vibrant private sectors and a host of other productive and effective structures.

The foregoing is well summarised by A. Gambari in an essay titled 'The Challenges of Nation Building: The Case of Nigeria' when he says that ' since the time of Adam Smith, every serious nationalist and politician has come to know that the wealth of a nation is not based on the wealth and opulence of its rulers (strong men) but on the productivity and industriousness of its citizenry (which can only be attained by building strong institutions).

Hence, if Nigeria must be listed amongst advanced nations

of the world in the nearest future, it must as a matter of urgency join and adopt the worldwide trend and strategy of building functional institutions. This is because institutions are the roadmap to enthroning national productivity and economic viability.

BUILDING STRONG INSTITUTIONS

One way we can build strong institutions in Nigeria is by reviewing the way our existing institutions function.

There is this popular saying that "You will keep getting the same result, if you keep doing things the same way". Modifying institutions usually involves actions predicated on three elements, which are: the rules, the enforcement characteristics and the norms of behaviour.

Today in our country, anti-corruption agencies and watchdog institutions have become toothless bulldogs; sometimes barking but definitely unable to bite. The primary reason for this is that the men manning these institutions were either recommended or influenced into power by one strong man in the country or they are strong men themselves. This has inevitably led to violation of codes of conduct, affected the transparent discharge of duties, hindered the course of justice and stalled the wheel of development and progress in the country.

For progress to be made therefore, the idea of celebrating strong men in their crafty ways should be jettisoned. Armed with the catalyst of a good value system, the masses must rise up to seek change in the country by questioning irregularities engineered by strong men at whatever level. This way, Nigeria will become more viable and vibrant in all ramifications of progress. Building of strong structures will foster political stability, ethnic harmony, religious tolerance and economic boom.

As we continue with a deep reflection on the realities plaguing

Nigeria, there are certain key areas where I believe we need to quickly rebuild our national institutions to prevent total collapse of our national heritage.

One key area that Nigeria has enthroned strong men over structure is leadership. Since the attainment of independence, Nigeria has constantly battled with the problem of raising a working leadership structure. A careful x-ray of post-independence Nigeria shows that Nigerian leaders are only concerned with what they can get for themselves first and later their region at the expense of national growth. What we need is a leadership structure that is devoid of ethnic dichotomies, profligacy, lawlessness, impunity, and corrupt practices.

One factor that has acted as a clog in the process of enthroning purposeful leaders, apart from the wrong value system of the general citizenry, is the godfather syndrome. It is a malaise that has been entrenched in the very soul of the nation's politics, and indeed, our national life in Nigeria. Since independence, Nigeria has experienced chaos of various kinds orchestrated by godfathers. These godfathers are people who see themselves as kingmakers. They are men who take decisions and have elected office holders at their beck and call.

> **Today in the Nigerian political space, politicians prefer to pay loyalty to their godfathers instead of engaging in projects that will improve the quality of the lives of the masses.**

Mind you, a corruptly-elected government will not deliver anything short of corruption, impunity, embezzlement and policies that are beneficial to the cabal of strong men, but inimical to the general welfare of the populace.

Another area in which we need to build strong structure is in our political system and mode of politicking. Considering the high rate of carpet-crossing, assassination, vulgarity and the sham multi-party configuration in our democracy, one is tempted to question the integrity of our politicians and the fate of our democratic process with such attitude and behaviours.

The beauty of democracy is inherent in the high level of competition amongst political parties. The situations we witnessed in the period before, during and after the last elections clearly show that Nigeria is tilting more towards a one party system and that the ruling party is a place everybody wants to belong because of the selfish ambition for political largesse and relevance. This ought not to be.

In my view, Nigeria should adopt a two or three party system. Under this system, the excesses, actions and inactions of leaders will be appropriately checked. Apparently, for some years now, out of the several registered parties in Nigeria only two are really visible. I now ask, of what importance is keeping so many parties without any meaningful impact?

More importantly, the hate-game, mudslinging, witch-hunting, vendetta, and other such shenanigans against one's political opponents should be avoided as politics is not a 'do or die' affair. Frankly speaking, the way and manner our politicians have gone about with the game of politics is worrisome and of damaging effect on national progress. Today, the man that is not carrying the card of the ruling party becomes a target for victimization, oppression and attack in whatever capacity possible. On the other hand, having the party card has become a license or ticket for perpetuating crimes and going scot free or unscathed. It has become a passport to partaking in the national cake, contracts, appointment, awards, and other such benefits.

We must not allow party politics, class affiliation and godfatherism to distract and rob us of achieving the utmost dream of becoming a strong nation which other nations can emulate. We should pay adequate attention to building an enviable nation with viable institutions.

The other area we need to look into is our economy. As a nation, we need to build a strong economic structure. Nigeria unarguably is a nation with gifted men and women. All we need to realise our dream of entering the fold of advanced nations is a national economic plan.

There is a need to look inwards to find ways to develop our economy. We have all that is needed to thrive in every sector of our national life. Let's develop economic policies, make effective economic laws, and reduce our dependence on other nations to the barest minimum.

> **I am deeply concerned that some of the things we import (toothpicks for example) are things that we are capable of producing. It is high time we awoke the giant in us to boost our economy and drive our nation to where it ought to be.**

We can achieve this by encouraging promising initiatives and start seeking solutions to the issues plaguing us economically.

Enough of the total dependence on oil; it is time to diversify our economy. It is time to open more channels of wealth and economic buoyancy. We must also concentrate on raising technocrats and experts and make sure these are placed in strategic positions to help us build strong national institutions rather than strong men, because strong men definitely don't last.

I have no doubt that when the above suggestions are put into work that Nigeria will become a better place for us all. Unless the aforesaid are taken into cognisance, all attempts to come to par with super nations technologically, politically, economically and otherwise will forever remain a mirage.

Once again, let's remind ourselves as Nigerians that rather than seeking or depending on strong men to change the fortunes of our nation and the fate of its people, we must be mindful that we hold the greater power to determine the destiny of our nation. Let me conclude by referring once more to a statement made by President Obama at the event I cited earlier in the chapter:

"The world will be what you make of it. You have the power to hold your leaders accountable, and to build institutions that serve the people. You can serve in your communities, and harness your energy and education to create new wealth and build new connections to the world. You can conquer disease, and end conflicts, and make change from the bottom up. You can do that. Yes you can because in this moment, history is on the move. But these things can only be done if all of you take responsibility for your future."

I hope we take these words seriously and act on them. We are the change we seek.

GOLDEN TRUTHS
FROM CHAPTER 10

- No society can develop beyond the level of the workable institutions it has put in place.

- Nigeria has concentrated more on building strong men than strong institutions, such that the men have become much stronger than the institutions.

- All developed nations of the world have ceased to depend on strong leaders because they have built strong institutions over the years.

- Nigerians can build strong institutions by reviewing and improving the way the existing ones function.

- Nigeria must look inwards to find ways of developing every sector of its economy, rather than depending on importation or foreign support.

11

THE NECESSITY FOR NATIONAL RE-ORIENTATION ON VALUES

"The trouble with Nigeria is simply and squarely a failure of leadership. There is nothing basically wrong with the Nigerian character. There is nothing wrong with the Nigerian land or climate or water or air or anything else. The Nigerian problem is the unwillingness or inability of its leaders to rise to the responsibility, to the challenge of personal example which are the hallmarks of true leadership."

—Chinua Achebe

This quotation has been cited once in this book. It is probably the most popularly known statement on the failure of leadership in Nigeria as a country. That is why I feel that we will never be able to effectively address and redress the question of leadership in Nigeria without taking a closer look at this statement that is credited to one of Nigeria's most illustrious sons. I have also used several other quotations in this book from Chinua Achebe which should go a long way to tell of my respect and honor to the man and his talent.

However, when it comes to this question of leadership, this is one area where I will beg to disagree with the doyen of Nigerian literature.

Let's examine his statement in detail.

Chinua Achebe wrote *"…there is nothing basically wrong with the Nigerian character. . . "*

Really? As a patriotic citizen of Nigeria myself I can easily understand where Chinua Achebe is coming from when he says there is nothing basically wrong with the Nigerian character. When I read such a statement from him or any other Nigerian, I cannot but be sympathetic to their cause. The truth however is far from that statement. There are many things basically wrong with the Nigerian character. Many of these things have been enumerated in this book.

The things that are wrong with our national character are not just the things that are being manifested today; many things have been wrong for a long time before now.

Let's face it. We as Nigerians have issues that we must address in regards to our character and behaviors in general.

> **I'm sorry, I am not such a romantic believer as our literary icon. I will rather be a pragmatic realist than a romantic believer. It is my belief that if we don't face who we are and tell ourselves the way it is, we will only be chasing mirage when it comes to the issues of national development and transformation.**

It is like a sick man that does not admit his diagnosis, comforting himself that he is well when all can clearly see the symptoms of his sickness. We Nigerians have character issues. Until we admit this, we will not be in the position to address the issues; but once we admit it, we could take courage to face the problem and overcome our demons.

The notion that there is nothing basically wrong with the Nigerian character cannot be right by any means. Do you mean there was nothing wrong with the basics of our character when:

1. Our people were making human sacrifices before the emergence of missionaries on our land?
2. Most of our people were killing and murdering twin babies?
3. Our people will bury innocent citizens with their deceased kings?
4. Our elites and aristocrats sold their fellow men into slavery in their millions?
5. The rulers owned everything and the citizens owned close to nothing?
6. Our people would marry 3, 4, 5, 20 or more wives?
7. Our people would force their daughters to go through the rituals of circumcision?
8. Tribes and people groups annihilated other groups just because of some flimsy excuses?
9. Some of our people actually practiced cannibalism?
10. Our politicians easily amass to themselves the wealth of their people while the rest of the populace live in abject poverty?
11. Students and ordinary citizens are bragging about getting an opportunity to eat of the national cake?
12. We need "long leg" and connection before we can get

matters of significance resolved?

13. Our people are willing to take other people's lives to make money rituals?

14. People are more afraid of witches and wizards than the God of heaven?

15. Parents, families and relatives send their children for prostitution abroad?

16. Our people are willing to traffic drugs that kill other people, both within and outside the country, just for them to make money?

17. Parents bribe their way for their children to get admission into higher institutions?

18. Exam malpractice is so rampant among our students?

19. Advanced fee fraud (419) originated from our country?

20. Children are ready to sacrifice their parents and parents ready to sacrifice their children just to have money, fame or wealth?

The list of those things that are wrong with the basic character of our people cannot be exhausted in this book. We all know most of them. I already referred to this when I highlighted the corrupt value system of our people. We need to address it, we need to face it. Every nation under the sun has its own issues. Those countries that have faced their issues and challenge themselves to change are those we now call civilized countries. We want to run to these societies because they have faced and challenged their demons. They have admitted their faults and have changed their ways; hence they were able to build progressive and prosperous societies that everyone of us would rather go and live in today.

As I have said earlier, our leaders are only a reflection of who we are as a people. If the vices I mentioned above and more had not been so prevalent in our nation and character, there was no way we would have produced leaders with these evils.

> We produce leaders with corrupt tendencies only because we as a nation practice these things. It's not just our leaders who exhibit corrupt practices. Before our leaders did, our peoples did.

It is now the time for a new generation of Nigerians and indeed Africans to arise and confront all the wrongs, evils and corrupt practices in their culture. For us to build a better future, we must admit those things that are wrong in our society and aggressively fight to eradicate them from our national consciousness.

We know that whenever we notice that our land is not as fertile as we want it to be, we get fertilizers for it. When our weather condition is not as conducive as we would like it to be, we install air conditioners and fans in our houses. When thousands die from fever or cholera because of our bad water, we subject it to hygienic processing through sodium dioxide and filtration for purification. When we discover that our air is polluted, we find ways of purifying it so that it does not become poisonous for our people. What I am trying to say is that there is nothing wrong to admit that we have bad land, climate, water, air, etc.

Israel is a great example of this. God has used them to prove to us that you could be established in a land that was once absolutely useless and detestable. Because the Israelis admitted their challenges, they were able to surmount them. This has made Israel one of the most fertile and most productive lands in the world today.

The issue is not for us to bury our heads in the sand like ostriches and say nothing is wrong with our character, land, air, water, etc. The victory comes only when we remove our heads from the sand and admit our faults, face our challenges.

As a believer and pastor, I know for sure that the human nature is basically sinful. As a result, we all need redemption. It is this acknowledgment that forms the basis of the Christian faith. We are all wrong; no one knows how to do right. No one can do what is right in his own power or strength. We all need redemption. We all need reformation. We are all in need of regeneration, both as individuals and as a nation. Admission of guilt – that is the beginning of our process of change and transformation.

TEMPLATES ON VALUE RE-ORIENTATION

Interestingly, in recent times, there have been calls from different corners of the country, emphasising the need for value re-orientation with the ultimate goal of national transformation. One of this was the Kuru Declaration of 2001. During the fourth retreat of Ministers and Permanent Secretaries at the Institute for Policy and Strategic Studies in Jos that took place from February 23 to 25 2001, under the regime of President Olusegun Obasanjo, a 12-point declaration, popularly called the Kuru Declaration, was made.

The high points in this declaration show clearly the need for national re-orientation as a response to increasing level of depreciation in our moral and national values. It is strikingly sad that a good number of Nigerians are not even aware of this declaration, not to talk of imbibing its tenets. Let me reproduce it here:

THE KURU DECLARATION

- We subscribe to the New National Ideology, which is, to build a truly great African democratic country, politically united, integrated and stable, economically prosperous, socially organized, with equal opportunity for all, and responsibility from all, to become the catalyst of African Renaissance, and making adequate all-embracing contributions, sub-regionally, regionally and globally.

- We adopt the New Orientation as an agenda for dealing with immediate and future issues of governance of Nigeria; removing impediments to efficiency and effective implementation and execution of programs initiated by the Federal Government; Expeditious actualization of government objectives and vision of national renewal and re-construction.

- We rededicate ourselves and those who serve under us to the values of patriotism, honesty, hard work, and diligence, merit and excellence, trustworthiness, personal discipline, tolerance and mutual respect, justice and fairness, love, care and compassion.

- We pledge to eschew corruption, slothfulness, nepotism, indiscipline, bitterness, prejudice and other manifestoes of anti-social behaviour.

- We shall undertake a critical review of practices and procedures in every Department of Government, so as to rapidly increase their productivity and service delivery to the public.

- We shall foster a culture of efficiency in the management of funds and other resources; maintaining high standards of resource management; and reducing waste at all times.

- We shall efficiently supervise all Government Department and Agencies, ensuring timely returns and reports, and undertaking regular spot checks.

- We shall abide by the terms of the Code of Conduct which we all have signed, as expression of our commitment to the crusade against corruption, and working closely with all relevant agencies such as the independent Corruption Practices and other Related Offences Commission, the Code of Conduct Bureau and the Public Complaints Commission.

- We undertake to strengthen the partnership in working with the private sector, since this partnership translates to a better appreciation of the wealth-creating capacity of this sector, and the need for Government, through its various ministries and legislative processes create an enabling environment for the sector to function efficiently as the major driver of the economy.

- We shall strive to strengthen and inculcate the culture of working closely and in consultation with the leadership of labour and civil society organisations.

- We shall mobilise, involve and promote the interest of all stakeholders, namely, the society in general; since in the ultimate, all decisions and actions of government are aimed at the promotion of public welfare, there is also the need for a new attitude that has welfare permanently in focus, as the only goal, and the economic well-being of all citizens, under unfettered freedom, is of cardinal importance; and we shall design strategies and techniques of implementation for the New Orientation so as to ensure that the values being inculcated permeate all levels of management and staff. (Source: Eric Teniola, Vanguard News, July 29, 2015).

Subsequently after this, other government reforms like NEEDS (National Economic Empowerment and Development Strategy) in 2004, and the 2009 Re-Branding project by the late Prof. Dora Akunyili, the then Minister of Information had value re-orientation as one of their primary goals.

BEYOND PAPERWORK

However, looking at the prevailing values, attitudes and behavioural patterns in our country, we cannot deny that while there appears to be so much on paper, there has been no significant change in our mentalities. This clearly shows that we need to go beyond mere paper reforms and declarations and move higher to the level of implementation and inculcation. Until we each pursue value re-orientation with all vigour, we will never be able to achieve much as a nation.

As I already mentioned, the task of collective national re-orientation must begin at the level of instilling the good values we wish to project as a nation into our children and youths. More importantly, every Nigerian must resolve that social sins highlighted by men like Mahatma Ghandi must be eradicated in the country. These are: wealth without work, pleasure without conscience, science without humanity, knowledge without character, politics without principle, commerce without morality and worship without sacrifice. More so, crimes and offences should be punished to serve as a deterrent to others. Hard work should be rewarded and only men and women of integrity should be elected/appointed to leadership positions.

We should begin to shift our gaze from materialism and wealth accumulation to pursue values of honesty, dedication and honour. Political positions should not be equated with fat salaries and embezzlement but it should be a service to humanity; until the remuneration of political office holders are drastically reduced to be at par with that of civil servants, we might not be able to bring in sanity to that section of the nation. When agencies like ICPC and EFCC do their job without fear or favour, Nigerians will know that the government means business.

This is a wakeup call to Nigerians. We cannot continue to

trade blames at this point. We have to take responsibility for our wrongdoings and choose to stand for what is right. When I stand for the right and you stand for the right, in no time, our values will change for the better, our country will witness huge developments and our image will be redeemed.

IS NIGERIA READY TO GO FROM THE THIRD WORLD TO THE FIRST WORLD?

A leader that Nigerians like to refer to and quote in recent times has been Lee Kuan Yew of Singapore. Nigerians like to use the example of how Singapore moved from a third world country to a first world nation in one generation. Unfortunately, these teachers and demagogues don't usually tell us how Lee Kuan Yew managed to achieve his feat.

Lee Kuan Yew, like no other man, understood the importance of altering the value system of a nation before trying to make that nation a great nation. He understood that nations and peoples are not great by the virtue of their wealth; they are only great by the wealth of their virtues.

So, as a matter of urgency, Lee Kuan Yew in Singapore embarked on a journey to aggressively enforce a godly value system in the society. He did this by instilling in the culture of the people a strict system of penalties. The penal system of Singapore is only rivaled by those of some of the Muslim nations of the Middle East.

Briefly, we shall have a look at some of the penalties in the Singapore society. Incidentally, even though some of these penalties were established decades ago, they are still being adhered to by the people of Singapore today because for forty years they were enforced by Lee Kuan Yew. So, when we admire the state of Singapore – their progress, stability, wealth, prosperity and sound value systems, we should know that these things don't just fall from the sky; they must be introduced and enforced by somebody. This therefore must be the role of a remnant leader.

Lee Kuan Yew was a remnant leader who understood the importance of value systems in developing a nation.

> **If we want to build a nation that will have a successive history of growth, development and prosperity, we must begin to pay attention to not just economic facts and systems, but to the relevance and importance of value systems as well.**

Here are some of the penalties for civil disobedience in Singapore:

1. If you are caught chewing gum, you are penalized. You pay a fine of $1000 or a year in prison.
2. If you cross the road in the wrong place, you are going to be penalized because you did not act by the truth. You pay a fine of $200.
3. If you are found littering the place by throwing bottles or paper on the ground, you are either imprisoned or heavily fined $800 dollars.
4. If you are caught spitting or defecating in public, you are penalized with prison sentence or a heavy fine.
5. If you are caught throwing a cigarette butt, you would be penalized with similar punishment. $1000 as a first offender and $5000 for repeat offender.
6. If you are caught with illegal drugs, you are sentenced to

death.

7. Eating in public transportation or smoking at an outdoor bus stop incurs fines, ranging from $500 – $1000.

8. If you are caught vandalizing, like making graffiti, you are caned - up to 24 strokes on your bare buttocks.

9. If you use the public toilet and do not flush it after yourself, you will be caned.

10. If you walk about undressed or nude, even in your own house, you would be heavily penalized. If you hug in public without permission you would be penalized.

11. If you criticize other religions, you are going to prison.

12. If you tell lies, for example, introducing a stranger as your friend, it is considered deception and you go to jail.

13. If you log on to an Internet connection that you have not paid for. It is considered hacking and you have to pay for it. It attracts $5000 fine.

14. If you are caught in unlawful sexual relationship, you get 2 years imprisonment.

15. Mutiny, discharge of firearm, treason, murder are punishable by death.

16. Robbery is punishable by caning and prison sentence.

17. Driving under the influence of alcohol is punishable by hefty fines and prison term.

18. Piracy is punishable by a fine of $1000

19. Theft and shoplifting are punishable by heavy fines.

20. Racism attracts heavy penalties.

ARE WE READY TO BECOME A SINGAPORE?

Now, I will like to look in the face of those people who use Singapore as an example for Nigeria. How many of them will approve of such measures as listed above? We all as a people need to learn afresh to live orderly. We must learn to live right. As drastic as these measures are, I can understand where Lee Kuan Yew was coming from because for a society to go from an extreme level of disorganization to an orderly, organized and structured society as Singapore is today, sometimes you will need to go from one extreme to the other before you find a middle ground. This is the principle of pendulum swing.

No matter what anyone thinks of the measures above, the results cannot be denied. All lovers of freedom and democracy all over the world criticize any country they want to, but leave Singapore alone because Singapore has more results to show than all those countries that are criticizing others for lack of freedom and democracy.

> **Results silence the mouths of the critics. Let's bring our society to a place where we will begin to have results first. To get there we need more than statistics. We need more than raw material. We need more than university education. We need an entrenchment of strong value systems that are godly and veritable.**

We can only be great by the wealth of our virtues before we will become great by the virtue of our wealth.

The question now is, is the Nigerian populace ready for the change they are clamoring for? Will the Nigerian populace tolerate a leader like Lee Kuan Yew? Will they embrace such measures as we have seen above to be implemented in Nigeria today? Won't we use the flimsy arguments of freedom of speech and democracy to kill such an initiative, if not such remnant leader himself?

Are we really serious about change? How serious are we? How serious is our new government about change? How serious is our senate and House of Representatives about change? Remember that these changes must not only affect the leaders and rulers of the nation. Granted that it must start with them; but it must go beyond them to reach every citizen of the land. Until there is a drastic change in the citizenry, there is no hope for any nation.

Even in cases of remnant leaders like Awolowo and Obasanjo, the stories will always repeat themselves as soon as they leave the stage. An unclean pot will keep on reproducing an unclean content. If the value systems of Nigeria and Nigerians don't change, we will keep on recycling and reproducing only those types of leaders we are seeing so far. Miracles will not happen, even in cases of remnant leaders.

The only thing that can bring a lasting change to our leadership failure is to go down to the grassroots and change the whole faulty and corrupt value system of our people.

GOLDEN TRUTHS
FROM CHAPTER 11

- It is not true that the Nigerian character is without flaw.

- To make progress as a nation, we must be ready to admit and address our faults, just as some other nations did before becoming developed.

- Good national values must be constantly communicated to citizens right from childhood.

- If Nigeria is to enjoy the same rapid and extraordinary transformation that Singapore had, then Nigerians must be willing to pay the same price of discipline, commitment and patriotism that the Singaporeans paid.

12

GOOD NATIONAL VALUES PRODUCE GOOD NATIONAL LEADERS

When your values are clear to you, making decisions becomes easier.

—**Roy E. Disney**

Now that we have seen the need for us to have new sets of values as a nation, it is good for us to also realize that it is good sets of values that will produce good national leaders needed to move the nation forward. This is because, in any generation, those who eventually emerge as leaders in whatever capacity always emerge from the people. Therefore, if the citizens share or exhibit values that are inimical to the ideals of national unity or nation building, then how do we expect those who emerge to lead the nation to show values that are different? As the saying goes, "a people deserve the kind of leaders they get." In many respects, the leadership reflects the people.

Leaders are neither angels nor spirits. They live and grow from among the people; their existence is given expression and influenced by happenings in the environment where they live. Expecting leaders who live in a largely corrupt and morally lax society to live above board while shying away from the urgent task to change and orientate the citizenry will only amount to putting the cart before the horse.

HOW NATIONAL VALUES INFLUENCE LEADERSHIP

The greatest challenge for Nigerians who desire to see a changed society is to focus first on their value systems as a people. If the value systems of the citizens are right, they would not select corrupt or bad leaders. For example, in societies where there are good moral values, people would not elect corrupt politicians or collect money to get the wrong people into office. Even if a corrupt politician finds his way by hook or by crook into the government, since the moral values of the masses contradict the corrupt values of the politician, he would be exposed and easily dismissed.

Therefore what we need in Nigeria and Africa in general is not just a good leader, but a good set of virtues and good value systems in the masses that would make them abhor and reject any manifestation of corruption in their leaders and would-be leaders.

Writing on his blog, Ojeniyi Ayokunnu puts it beautifully when he states that, "Economic reforms are good but not good enough to change a nation. Any nation that would indeed be great must be established upon enduring national values that bind every individual in the corporate entity... Corruption is referred to as the bane of development in Nigeria but we often forget same does not exist by itself. What we lack as a nation is a system of values and nothing else".

I quite agree with him that no matter the economic policy or reforms undertaken by the government we will never make much meaningful progress nor attain our full potentials if we do not progressively and persistently pursue the implementation of a sound national value system.

Thus, we should not expect, and we will not have the kind of improvements or the leadership that we seek as a nation if we don't work on our value system. For example, under the late Umaru Musa Yar Adua's administration, there was a bold step made towards changing the negative perception of Nigeria both locally and internationally through the Rebranding Project. Unfortunately, this brilliant program failed to achieve its set objectives because it did not first attempt to establish and promote good national values in the citizens.

> **The level, direction or type of transformation any country experiences will always depend largely on the individual values of its citizens and the national values expounded by the nation and its leaders.**

Consequently, it is imperative that we begin an urgent reorientation of our people and ourselves. We must begin to define what describes our existence as a people, as a nation. What core values do we want as a nation? We must inculcate values that will promote national unity and integration.

National values are core principles ingrained into the mental and social structures of a society, which help to dictate the action and behaviour of the citizenry. These are qualities, principles and behaviours every nation hold in high esteem as it seeks to achieve its ultimate objectives.

Stating the importance of a national value system, an author explains that "The values an individual or a community or even a nation live by determine the individual's or community's way patterns of existence and general orientation to life. The same is true of a nation. A national philosophy is the basis of a nation's program in all aspects of her existence as a nation."

For me, elements that should make up the mainstay of our national values should include concepts such as national unity, patriotism, dignity of labour, honesty and education. I strongly hold the opinion that one of the most essential elements that we need to consciously and comprehensively inject into the blood stream of our national existence, as a national value is national unity. As I have stated earlier in this book, God allowed everything that happened in the amalgamation of 1914 for a specific purpose. There is no gainsaying that the different ethnic nationalities that make up Nigeria are better off together as a single entity. Consequently, Nigerians must begin to see themselves first as Nigerians and not as tribal or ethnic entities. This is one of the crucial way leaders can be selected based on merit, and not on sentiments.

Evidence that Nigerians are not presently united as a nation can be gleaned from their comments and conversations on social media and on the websites of national newspapers. The continuous claim of government neglect and marginalisation by some parts of the country, the current agitation for the actualization of a sovereign state of Biafra by some persons from the eastern part of the country, the existence of such groups as OPC, MASSOB, ACF, Boko Haram, IPOB, Radio Biafra and the fact that we have consistently failed to understand ourselves only underscore the reality that Nigerians are not united yet. How then can we have the nation of our dreams?

In a plural and heterogeneous society such as ours, tribal prejudice and ethnic divisions only elevate wrong sentiments above the greater good of the nation, thereby triggering disunity, hampering national development and producing dysfunctional leadership.

Another fundamental core value I believe we need to set in place in the nation to produce quality leadership is patriotism and loyalty. I believe that the lack of these is what has led to the abuse and misuse of opportunities by many of our past leaders. Patriotism is the love and devotion a person has for his country, and loyalty is the support and allegiance he gives to it. This embodies the spirit of nationalism, which places national interest over personal, parochial or ethnic sentiments. It is the belief that the nation comes first before any other thing or person.

Presently, the spirit of patriotism is conspicuously missing among the citizenry and the political elite, and thus affecting those who have the reins of leadership in the nation. Undoubtedly, history has shown that only few leaders in the annals of the country were ready to sacrifice their lives, or even their comforts to better the lot of the country. What we have witnessed most of the time is the blatant and enormous exploitation of the country's resources for personal gratification to the detriment of the nation and the citizenry.

Honesty is another element I believe is relevant to the survival of our nationhood. Honesty is the quality of being morally upright. It is a state of the heart that denotes truthfulness, straightforwardness, fairness, and the absence of theft or cheating or any form of double standard. In many civilised and developed societies, you don't need to be a pastor or a prophet before people believe or take you at your word. This is because of the culture of honesty that has been implanted into the national conscience of such societies. Unfortunately, in our case, it is not so.

It is quite sad and regrettable that we live in a country where riches and wealth have been so much emphasized that people now worship money and materialism.

Many Nigerians, especially the youths chase riches and wealth at all cost. To them this seems to be the greatest thing or achievement in life, because the society celebrates the rich (irrespective of how they got their wealth) and despise the poor. Consequently, people will engage in all forms of social vices in order to get wealth. Such vices include armed robbery, human and drug trafficking, kidnapping, embezzlement of public funds, advanced fee fraud, prostitution, and assassination. In this kind of avaricious and materialistic setting, honesty no doubt is the first casualty. And as this trend is allowed to fester, leaders soon emerge from the same corrupt seedbed and we expect such leaders to be saints!

> **We must also orientate our people on the dignity of labour. As a matter of urgency, we must de-emphasize and seek to eradicate the get-rich-quick-by-whatever-means mentality of our people and replace it with the consciousness of dignity of labour.**

Citizens must know and see that there is dignity in labour. They must be made to understand that they have a duty, a responsibility to work for pay; money must be earned and rightly too. When such values are in place, we will hardly find incidents of people seeing public offices as avenues for looting and embezzlement. It will hardly occur that public office holders are diverting public funds or allocating unjustified allowances and privileges to themselves.

The value and need for tolerance in our nation cannot be over-emphasized. The reason we have continued to witness and experience inter-tribal conflicts and religious crises in our dear nation is no doubt lack of tolerance among us. This is also why we have leaders who have been openly partisan, favouring only members of their political parties, ethnic groups or religions. Many Nigerians have become so religiously fanatical that they have no love lost for those who practice any religion different from theirs. Some are drawn into a cold war with others simply because they do not share the same opinion on national or religious issues. This is not only uncivilized but also unacceptable in a nation that is seeking national advancement and progressive leadership.

This is why the virtue of tolerance must be inscribed on the table of the nation's conscience as a vital national value, which must be exhibited by every citizen of the country. Nigerians must learn to accommodate the opinions, religions and perspectives of others irrespective of the ethnic division, religious affiliation or socio-cultural differences. This is definitely the way to go if we desire the birth of a new nation every one of us would be proud of. It is the only way we can get leaders who will not be paranoid of constructive criticisms or oppressive towards people perceived not to be in agreement with their programs or policies.

Again, is it not true that, as a result of the faulty, lopsided and negative values that Nigerians have imbibed over the years, we have lost our respect for human life? The mortality rate in Nigeria has gone so high because we have no regard for life. Death seems to mean nothing to us anymore. People are kidnapped regularly, many of whom are never seen again because they have been killed and used for ritual purposes. Yet nobody seems to bother, except a few immediate family members of the victims. Sometimes, we walk by corpses on our highways and streets and very few bother to ponder on the abnormality of such in a sane society. On our streets are beggars with putrefying sores, mad men and women endangering their lives by feeding on filth and sleeping in sewers and we are not concerned. How then do we expect to produce leaders who are sensitive to the plight of the masses?

If the masses are desensitised to their own sufferings, from where would a considerate leader emerge? This is the reason I believe that respect for human life should be one of the core values of our nation. It is this that gives us our humanity.

Liberty and freedom should be one of the most guaranteed rights of every individual citizen. And every citizen must know, embrace and appreciate this – not just for themselves but for every other person around them. This should not only be enshrined in the constitution, it should be a way of life because it is the desire of every human. Patrick Henry, an influential figure in the American Revolution, once said "is life so dear, or peace so sweet, as to be purchased at the price of and chains and slavery? Forbid it Almighty God! I know not what course others may take; but as for me, give me liberty or give me death!" This statement underscores the vital importance of freedom and liberty to the peaceful existence of a nation.

Every citizen should be free to think, speak, make choices and act as he chooses without any external interference, irrespective of who agrees with him or not, and of course as long as it doesn't infringe upon the freedom and liberty of others. We must shun the culture of attacking or enslaving people we consider inferior or taking advantage of the helpless.

|| **If we see the culture of abusing and maltreating others around us as normal, then we cannot expect a leader who celebrates the liberty and freedom of his citizens!** ||

Respect for the rule of law should be another virtue that every citizen of our nation, irrespective of social status, must abide by; everyone must be equal before the law. The rule of law presupposes the supremacy of the law of the land over every other personality, group or institution. Activities and policies by individuals or the government must be guided by the rule of law. The rule of law is what sets a civilised nation apart from the uncivilized. Consequently, every effort must be made to make sure the rule of law is respected, as this will ensure good governance and accountability.

Education is key for any nation willing to produce quality leadership and an informed citizenry. It is so sad that we have come to a point in our national life that we place so little emphasis on education either on a personal or on a national scale. Even when we claim to get education, the standard is so low that it becomes unprofitable in the long run. How then do we produce enlightened leaders? We cannot continue like this. Education makes it impossible to enslave the people because it enlightens people, and helps to preserve our values. Consequently, there is a need for a national reorientation on the value of education in our country.

One other value that I think we should inculcate is taking responsibility for our lives and destinies, rather than sheepishly waiting for things to change by themselves or by the "magic wand" of an exceptional leader. Nigerians must understand the need to intelligently and consistently express their wishes and concerns to the government, instead of murmuring in the privacy of their rooms and resigning to "fate" when things are not being done properly, whether in our localities or in the nation as a whole.

GOLDEN TRUTHS
FROM CHAPTER 12

- Leaders are often products and reflections of their environments.

- Where citizens imbibe and uphold good national values, it is practically impossible to select corrupt leaders.

- Attempts at rebranding Nigeria's image before the international community have failed because efforts are not first put into instilling national values in the citizenry.

- Elements that should make up the mainstay of our national values should include concepts such as national unity, patriotism, dignity of labour, honesty and education.

13

BUILDING STRONG STRUCTURES AND INSTITUTIONS FOR NIGERIA

•——•——•——◐◉◑——•——•——•

"Men may die, but the fabrics of free institutions remain unshaken."

—Chester A. Arthur

The hardship plaguing Nigeria and the depths of despair its current situation has created at the moment have continued to tug at my mind. Now that it is clear that what we need to do in the country is to build national institutions that will work and withstand any challenge, I'd like to now explore the ways by which we can build strong systems and institutions for Nigeria. Let it be stated that building strong systems and institutions is not an easy task anywhere. Just as there is no short-cut by which a baby can attain adulthood, so also there is no short route to attaining and building strong systems and institutions.

> **From time immemorial, every nation that has ever built a strong system and viable institutions did so through investment of time, resources, skills, ideas, patriotism, planning, strategy and goal setting into the process.**

For instance, in 1960, President John F. Kennedy of the United States called together scientists, heads of airlines and engineers and gave them an assignment: "land an American on the moon in the next ten years." Nobody had done it before. How they would do it, nobody knew. All they had was a goal and a promise of all they would need. They beat their target by one year and landed someone on the moon by 1969. Now this is what I call harnessing what you have in a nation - the technocrats, the experts, the intellectuals, to get what you want - a national institution, achievement and pride

It therefore implies that building a strong nation founded upon solid and viable structures and institutions can be achieved through an undaunted cross-fertilisation of ideas; institution and constitution of strong regulatory bodies to checkmate excesses in every sector; courage and selfless commitment to drive society on the path of greatness.

COMBATING CHALLENGES TO BUILDING STRONG NATIONAL STRUCTURES AND INSTITUTIONS

It is no longer strange that everywhere one turns in Nigeria, there are visible traits of institutional flaws and collapse. It therefore becomes quite evident that what Nigeria lacks are neither human nor natural resources but viable national institutions sufficiently equipped to carry the burdens of a heterogeneous nation such as Nigeria.

Over the years in Nigeria, sporadic attempts have been made to build strong national structures and institutions by successive governments, but suffice it to say that these attempts have met with variegated challenges, which have stalled the process or in some cases, made it experience absolute collapse. Let me quickly point your attention to some of these challenges. They include the following:

(1) Flawed leadership and followership. The leadership-followership pattern in the country is grossly flawed. The leaders in power have set very wrong precedents for the followers and the followers have perfectly imbibed their style, using them as measures for modeling their actions and inactions.

Striking and distressing is the fact that sometimes electoral officials saddled with the conduct of elections simply choose to dance to the rhythms of fraud and irregularities initiated by the power hungry and idea bereft politicians. So, let me begin my recommendations in this chapter by saying that it is imperative to improve on the mode of conducting elections in the country. Even though the last elections in the country were hailed as relatively free and fair, more still needs to be done. I must also note that while the recent introduction of the card reader helped a little in our electoral process, it was flawed with some irregularities. However, that is not to say that it cannot be used to conduct free, fair and credible elections.

The point I am trying to make is that the lapses detected in the previous elections must be reviewed to ensure more credible elections in the future. This is because, if the vote of the people counts through free and credible elections, it will give rise to trusted, purposeful, people-oriented leaders thereby engendering national progress and stability in all facets of our national life. It is through credible elections that we can fill the current leadership vacuum in Nigeria.

(2) Corruption. Corruption unarguably is the greatest threat to Nigeria's survival and progress. It has grown so big that it has become the symbol of our identity to the international community. According to Dike (1999) corruption is the only viable industry in Nigeria. This is because from the 'Ogas at the top' to the man on the street, there abounds corruption in different degrees in our society.

It therefore means that corruption exists in almost every segment of our nation. It is no longer a hidden reality that corruption is the major cause of Nigeria's failure to make meaningful progress in terms of quality of life of the citizens. Many viable institutions, programs and schemes, which were supposed to impact positively on the people were hijacked for selfish gains and diverted into the coffers of private individuals. Some of them were Operation Feed the Nation (OFN), Directorate of Food, Roads and Rural Infrastructure (DFRRI), The People's Bank of Nigeria (PBN), Better Life for Rural Women (BL), National Directorate of Employment (NDE), National Poverty Eradication Program (NAPEP) and others.

All these measures were supposedly meant to improve the quality of lives of the people but due to corruption, poor implementation, and wrong value system on the part of the citizens themselves, they ended largely in failure. What we see everywhere are indices of corruption. Therefore, if we must build strong national structures, then we must jettison attitudes, behaviours and value systems that have encouraged corruption over the years.

> **I call on the anti-corruption agencies in Nigeria - the Economic and Financial Crimes Commission (EFCC), the Independent Corrupt Practices Commission (ICPC) – to rise up to the expectations of Nigerians.**

The weakness of the various corruption agencies in the country has contributed to the prevalence of corruption in our nation. The agencies must be detached from government influence, interference and manipulation in the fight against corruption. More so, they must embark on an aggressive campaign against corrupt practices and leave no stone unturned in investigating allegations and even appearances of corruption.

In addition, our legal system has assisted in allowing corruption to fester in the country. The judiciary is supposed to be the hope of the common man. But today in Nigeria, it has become the jailer of the 'have nots' and exonerator of the 'well-to-do' in our society. Though not all legal practitioners are corrupt, it will not be out of place to say that quite a number of them have sacrificed truth and justice at the altar of corruption and greed in the discharge of their duties. The system must as a matter of necessity prioritize impartiality and fair play in delivering judgments.

(3) The quality of workers in the various sectors of our nation is also an encumbrance to building strong national structures. Today in Nigeria, incompetent and unqualified persons have been saddled with key responsibilities as a result of favouritism and on basis of who they are connected to. This has posed a serious hindrance to building strong national structures and institutions in Nigeria. Successive governments have upheld cronyism and ethnicity in the appointment of persons into key positions in several sectors, thereby engaging misfits and incompetent personnel to function in pivotal sectors of the economy.

(4) Mono-crop economy structure. Another major factor that has robbed Nigeria of strong national institutions is the over dependence on only one resource in determining the nation's revenue-expenditure profile and the balance of payment position. Prior to the discovery of oil in 1958, the major source of revenue was agriculture, but as soon as oil was discovered the agricultural sector was abandoned.

Agriculture is a key sector to the development of every nation. It contributes to the improvement of a nation's foreign exchange through exports as well as savings in import. The government should make the agriculture sector enterprising for youths to venture into by providing farmers intervention schemes, providing funds in form of loans and facilities to farmers. It will help reduce the high rate of unemployment ravaging our nation today.

(6) Weak private structures: The private sector in Nigeria is battling with several challenges as a result of harsh realities in the operating environment. The private sector should be enhanced to complement the effort of the government. The government must create an enabling environment for private firms to thrive. This can be achieved in clear terms through the policies that permit the operation of private firms, reduction in corporate taxes, improvement in security etc.

(7) Weak security system: Today, Nigeria is battling with diverse forms of security challenges such as gross lawlessness, soaring crime rate, armed insurgencies, factional fighting, kidnapping and a host of others. Considering the fragile nature of security at the moment in the nation, there is a dire need to beef up security in every region of the country; the kind that is captured by Imobighe when he said that, "security has to do with the freedom from danger, fear, anxiety or uncertainty. It is a condition of being protected from, or not being exposed to danger, (Imobighe: 2003, P. Vii). In doing this, there is a need for the government to sanitise and cleanse all the security units (Police, Army, Navy) of corrupt elements and practices. More so, the various security units must be well remunerated, constantly trained and their welfare and that of their family appropriately considered.

Also, the government of the day must tackle poverty, unemployment and the retrogressive value systems of the citizenry.

More importantly, we must see security as our business - everyone's business. We should be our brothers' keeper. Citizens must always report crimes and perpetrators of crime in whatever degree. Also, I believe that communal policing through community police and vigilantes should be encouraged.

Having discussed the challenges to building strong national structures and institutions, I will now talk more on the possible solutions and remedies.

First of all we must examine the causes of the great and traumatic failures of the past. This is the foundation on which the building of strong national institutions must be predicated. Since October 1, 1960, there have been series of socio-economic and political blunders, myriads of leadership flaws, as well as wrong value systems of the citizens that have created cracks in the wall of our national systems and institutions. Hence, to move forward and initiate a strong national system and institution, we must first know what the problems are, so as to address them squarely. More so, we should evolve a system that lays great emphasis on discipline and integrity. As a practical demonstration of this, we must ensure that only dependable and accountable men and women are appointed into political offices. These individuals must be of good reputation; they must be selfless technocrats and professionals - people who are not hungry for power or position just because of what they can get out of it.

But the citizens who will elect such men themselves must stop the habit of allowing themselves to be bribed, brainwashed or used by those who are out to sap the treasure of our nation. Then, we can enthrone great minds and leaders for our dear nation.

> **Furthermore, there should be systems for rewarding hard work and encouraging ideas suitable for national growth and progress.**

The absence of rewards and incentives for outstanding workers have in no small way affected the building of strong nation structures and institutions. If we are able to commensurately reward hard work, it will help to tame corrupt practices currently hindering progress in our nation. Inevitably, it will also motivate people to give their undivided loyalty to service in their duty post.

Lastly, the government should develop constructive and sound economic policies on agriculture, private sector growth, technological advancement and other areas that will help to diversify the nation's monolithic economy. The diversification from the economy will drastically reduce Nigeria's dependence on the outside world for her basic needs and bring her at par with world superpowers. This will save us of the pitfalls associated with over dependence on one resource to drive the economy.

Let me conclude this chapter by reaffirming my belief that

Building Strong Structures and Institutions for Nigeria

Nigeria is a great nation, and I am very optimistic and confident that in spite of the ups and downs we are currently facing, Nigeria will overcome in all spheres of human endeavours if both the leadership and the citizens of the country put their minds to it.

GOLDEN TRUTHS
FROM CHAPTER 13

- Attempts have been made by some past governments to build solid structures and institutions for Nigeria.

- Limitations on the part of the governments and uncooperative attitudes on the part of the citizens led to the failure or collapse of these structures and institutions.

- It is imperative to set up a credible electoral body that will facilitate, not frustrate, the voices of the people in their choice of leaders.

- Government must develop sound economic policies on agriculture.

14

RIGHTEOUSNESS EXALTS
A NATION

It is impossible to rightly govern the world without
God and the Bible

—George Washington

Having talked so much about the challenges that have
beset us over the years as a nation and the ways by
which we can rise above them, we now come to a
critical point in our discussion. It is pertinent for me to bring
to the fore a very fundamental dimension that is crucial to our
subject matter.

The Holy Bible makes an emphatic statement concerning the
secret of national greatness in Proverbs 14:34: *"Righteousness exalts
a nation, But sin is a reproach to any people."*

> **This simple declaration carries in it a profound truth, which I believe any nation seeking exaltation should consider diligently.**

This passage is not just an admonition to the nation of Israel but an instruction and a forewarning counsel to all nations on the earth, without distinction, and without exception. It is a universal principle.

The universal testimony of history attests to the veracity of the principle that the true greatness of a nation and that which determines the progress, peace and prosperity of its future lies not in the quality of its civilized population, nor its intellectual or technological advancement, nor yet in its political sagacity and tolerance; but in the quality of its moral rectitude in all its conducts, both in its private, public and international life as dictated by the will of God.

What this means is that in a nation's obedience to the instructions of God lies the strength and measure of its true greatness.

UNDERSTANDING RIGHTEOUSNESS AND SINFULNESS

As we consider this matter, we must first begin by critically looking at the terms. What is righteousness and what exactly is sin? Understanding these two concepts will help us to fathom the depths of truth recorded in the scripture verse above.

The dictionary definition of righteousness is the act of "always behaving according to a religious or moral code". By this definition righteousness implies a behaviour that is in conformity with accepted standards of morality, virtue, uprightness or justice.

The word righteous in the Hebrew implies being just, lawful, and correct. In the New Testament the word righteous comes from the Greek word *"dikaios"* which means observing divine laws or being upright and innocent.

Righteousness is the nature of God; God is righteous in all his ways and acts. Therefore, righteousness in biblical terms refers to being right with God or being in right standing with God. It is being fully obedient to God's commands and instructions.

The term "righteousness" as expressed in the Bible is only exhibited through conformity to God's standards. Since God is righteous and righteousness is His attribute in all things, He alone therefore becomes the standard of righteousness. His own nature, character and word become the only acceptable yardstick for measuring human righteousness not societal or traditional standards.

Sin, on the other hand, is acting contrary to the commandments or instructions of God. It is the opposite of righteousness; for as the scripture says in 1 John 3:4, "Whoever commits sin also commits lawlessness, and sin is lawlessness." This therefore means that sin is any disobedience to the nature and law of God. All sin (there is no small or great sin in the sight of God) is the rejection of God.

Righteousness is not what a man thinks is right or what a nation thinks is correct or appropriate. True righteousness is measured by what God says; it is what God thinks is right.

People want to choose their own paths. Nations want to set their own rules outside the perimeter of the will of God, but this is not the way to go.

The nature of fallen man will not allow him to do right by himself. Romans 7 says, "For the good that I will to do, I do not do; but the evil I will not to do, that I practice. Now if I do what I will not to do, it is no longer I who do it, but sin that dwells in me. I find then a law, that evil is present with me, the one who wills to do good." (verse 19- 21).

Even with the best of intentions, the moment we leave God out of the equation of our national development, we begin to stray from divine instruction and this leads to loss of influence and moral rectitude, which ultimately leads to the degradation and downfall of the individual or nation.

The popular idea today is that what is considered right depends on the individual. Some even point that there is neither right nor wrong, suggesting that truth is relative. But this is erroneous! God still dictates what is right; He changes not. God still makes the rules and He must make the rules. God still rules in the affairs of men; He is still in control of the universe:

> "And He changes the times and the seasons; He removes
> kings and raises up kings; He gives wisdom to the wise.
> And knowledge to those who have understanding."
> Daniel 2:21.

What is now left for us as individuals, or as a nation is to conform to his rules.

HOW RIGHTEOUSNESS EXALTS

> **So, when the Bible says that righteousness exalts a nation, it means that righteousness brings a country into favour with God who in turn lifts up such nation.**

Righteousness enhances the reputation, prosperity and exaltation of a nation. Righteousness lifts up a nation; it brightens its prospects and blesses its people.

Piety and righteousness always promote industry and honesty, and these are the things which bring divine security to a nation. These are the qualities that bring such nation into a place of honour. Explaining the usefulness of righteousness in a nation in his commentary on the whole Bible, Matthew Henry affirms that "a righteous administration of the government, impartial equity between man and man, public countenance given to religion, the general practice and profession of virtue, the protecting and preserving of virtuous men, charity and compassion to strangers ... these exalt a nation; they uphold the throne, elevate the people's minds, and qualify a nation for the favour of God, which will make them high, as a holy nation". But on the other way round sin brings disgrace to a people and makes them "despicable among their neighbours".

The children of Israel in Bible times were a classic example of a nation, which witnessed the two parts of these experiences. When they obeyed God and kept to His commandments they prospered and were exalted above their neighbours, so much that their fear fell upon the nations about them. But when they forsook God and disregarded His instructions, they fell into the hands

263

of their neighbours who oppressed and suppressed them with a mighty hand.

SECRET OF AMERICA'S GREATNESS

America became arguably the greatest nation in the world because of the fact that it was founded upon faith in God.

The statements of its founding founders, as well as religious expressions in its national symbols, national motto and even national anthem confirm this.

According to the 18th president of the United States, Ulysses S. Grant, "to the influence of this book (the Bible) we are indebted for the progress made in civilization, and to this we must look as our guide in the future". Andrew Jackson, the 7th president of America added to this position by saying that "It (the Bible) is the rock on which our republic rests". And lastly, from Thomas Jefferson, the third president of the US, and the author of the Declaration of Independence (1877), came the statement that "a studious perusal of the sacred volume will make better citizens, better fathers, and better husbands".

America's founding fathers were morally minded men guided by Christian principles gleaned from the Holy Bible. Unfortunately, it is clear to discerning Christians that America is beginning to lose its influence around the world because of its decline in moral rectitude and its blatant disregard for simple biblical principles and instructions it had once stood on.

HOW SIN DEBASES

Highlighting the consequences of sin in Psalms 107:34 the Bible reveals that God turns "A fruitful land into barrenness, For the wickedness of those who dwell in it." A naturally blessed and prosperous nation becomes a wilderness just because of sin. Can anyone deny that this is the lot of our nation, Nigeria? That sin is the real reason why a nation as divinely and naturally blessed as Nigeria has become an unfortunately barren and retrogressive wasteland? Can God's exclamation about Israel in Isaiah 1:4 not certainly be true of us as a nation?

"Alas, sinful nation,
A people laden with iniquity,
A brood of evildoers,
Children who are corrupters!
They have forsaken the Lord,
They have provoked to anger
The Holy One of Israel,
They have turned away backward."

Haven't we forsaken God? Haven't we become a nation full of iniquity, evildoers, corrupt people, and thus have provoked God to anger?

I do believe that the unchurched and unregenerate child of today is the criminal of tomorrow. When our youths and our children grow up without morals, without God, then the result is reproach upon the nation. When we rebel against God's standards, we move Him to provocation and dare His wrath. The moment we edge God out of our private lives and government activities, policies and programs, devastating retribution and destruction are the unavoidable consequences.

In Hosea 4:1-6, God had a controversy against Israel because they compromised His commandments and went their own ways. The warning God gave Israel about the consequences that would follow if they refused to allow His word govern the pattern of their lives and their national affairs is instructive to us today. A very clear fact from the passage is that sin brings natural and socio-economic devastation on a nation.

> **Disobedience to God and rebellion against God brings God's curse upon a nation. God withdraws his blessings and protection from a sinful nation, and the consequences are unimaginable.**

The moment God turns against a nation, every other thing takes a downward turn for the worse, even the natural environment. We must bring God back into the equation of our national lives. We must allow His words to form the foundation of our individual lives and civic laws.

THE CHURCH IN A SINFUL NATION

God expects the believers in a sinful nation to repent for the sins of the nation because He holds them responsible for the sins of the nation. In 2 Chronicles 7:14, God says "if My people who are called by My name will humble themselves, and pray and seek My face, and turn from their wicked ways, then I will hear from heaven, and will forgive their sin and heal their land.".

God was not talking to the unbelievers here; He was referring to "my people" these are believers! He was telling them that the condition in which He would heal their land was if they would humble themselves, repent, turn around, and seek His face! This places an enormous responsibility on the believers in Nigeria, and everywhere else in the world. Someone has rightly said, "As goes the church, so goes the nation".

Could it not be that the reason our country is in such a mess is because believers have forsaken God? Couldn't it be that it is because the church in Nigeria has failed in its responsibilities towards God and towards the nation that the country has degenerated into such abysmal condition and disgraceful status? Can we boldly say that church in Nigeria at the present hasn't forsaken God and His righteousness?

What Isaiah prophesied in scripture is true of many believers in this generation, "Therefore the Lord said: "Inasmuch as these people draw near with their mouths And honor Me with their lips, But have removed their hearts far from Me, And their fear toward Me is taught by the commandment of men" (Isaiah 29:13).

Candidly, this is the true state of the church of Christ in Nigeria. We have become so materialistic that we have even brought reproach to the name of Christ, the head of the church! No wonder we have lost the impact we ought to have in our nation, and in the world at large!

RETHINKING AND REPENTING AS A NATION

The Bible exhorts that corporate righteousness will bring honour and glory while corporate sin will bring a nation into disrepute and shame. We cannot deny the reality that sin has created our problems. How can a nation prosper with all the wickedness going on in it among the leaders and the led? With all the stealing, killings, immorality, rebellion, and other shenanigans shamefacedly committed in rebellion to the will of God, how dare we expect to prosper?

Sin will always bring reproach to us as individuals and as a corporate entity if it is not repented from. This is stark reality! And except we repent collectively and make a decision to align with God and His words in all aspects of our individual and national lives, things may continue to take a downward turn.

"Righteousness exalts a nation, but sin is a reproach to any people."

Let me conclude by saying, every nation deserves its leader, because leaders emerge from the populace. A righteous people would choose righteous leaders, but a corrupt people would be easily compromised into choosing corrupt politicians. Everything depends on the value system of the nation.

> **So, is leadership the biggest problem of Nigeria or Africa? My answer is No! Our faulty value system is where the problem is. Until we change the value system of the populace and the masses, we would always have bad leaders, and corrupt politicians.**

It does not matter how many years we wait. We have already waited for over 55 years. Another 500 years will not give us a better result than we presently have.

I therefore stand to call for a revolution of virtues, morals and values in our nation and continent. I hope our new government listens, but even more importantly I hope every conscientious Nigerian and African listens.

GOLDEN TRUTHS
FROM CHAPTER 14

- God's exhortation to righteousness is for all nations, not just the nation of Israel.

- In commitment to righteousness and moral rectitude lies the greatness of every nation.

- Righteousness means being in right standing before God.

- Sin is a violation of God's commandment.

- America became great because it was founded on faith in God.

- Nigeria must have a rethink and repent in order to experience God's visitation and enjoy His mercies and blessings!

FOR THE LOVE OF GOD, CHURCH AND NATION!

REFERENCES

CHAPTER ONE: TRACING THE BIRTH OF THE GIANT

- Ademoyega Adewale. 2014. Why We Struck. Ibadan: Evans Brothers Limited.
- Azikiwe Ifeoha. 2013. Nigeria: Echoes of a Century (Vol.1). Bloomington: Authorhouse
- Daily Times (1966, January 16). The Editorial Column.
- Laing Aislinn. May 29, 2015. Nigeria's President Goodluck Jonathan hands over to former dictator Muhammadu Buhari. The Telegraph. Retrieved July 31, 2015, from www.telegrsph.co.uk/news/worldnews/africaandindianocean/11637544/Nigerias-president-Goodluck-Jonathan-to-hand-over-to-former-dictator-Mohammadu-Buhari.html
- Madukwe Bartholomew (October 10, 2013). "Akinjide reveals genesis of Nigeria's problems". http://www.vanguardngr.com/2013/10/akinjide-reveals-genesis-nigerias-problems/
- Odeh E. Lemuel. Analysis of Factors Inhibiting Democracy and Democratization in Nigeria, 1999-2007. The Fourth Republic in Nigeria: A Decade of Democratisation Reviewed. Eds T. N. Sunday & T. Wauam Eds. Aboki Publishers: Makurdi.
- Ogbeidi M. Michael. 2012. Political Leadership and Corruption in Nigeria since 1960: A Socio-economic analysis. Journal of Nigeria Studies. Volume 1 no 2. Fall 2012.
- Omodia S.M. 2012. Election, Governance and the

Challenge of National Integration in the Nigerian Fourth Republic. British Journal of Arts and Social Sciences: British Journal Publishing, Inc. Vol.5 No.2: 2012

CHAPTER TWO: CONTEMPORARY NIGERIA: THINGS FALL APART

- Ademoyega Adewale 2014. Why we struck. Ibadan: Evans Brothers Limited.
- Afegbua Issa. 2014 Retrieved 10 July, 2015 fromhttp://chrisdonasco.blogspot.com/2014/12/conflicts-and-political-instability-in.html
- Ayobami O. Oyinola 2011. Corruption Eradication in Nigeria: An Appraisal. Retrieved 7 July, 2015 from http://www.webpages.uidaho.edu/~mbolin/ayobami.htm
- Transparency International. What is Corruption. Retrieved 6 July, 2015 fromhttp://www.transparency.org/what-is-corruption/
- British Broadcasting Corporation. July 30, 2007. "Rigging Nigeria" http://www.bbc.co.uk/radio4/history/document/document_20070730.shtml.
- Chido Nwangwu "Will religion be the time-bomb for Nigeria's latest transition to civilian rule?" US Africa Online. Retrieved 9 July, 2015 from http://www.usafricaonline.com/chido_religiouscrises.html
- Daily Independent editorial. 2014. " World bank Report on Poverty in Nigeria" Retrieved 7 July, 2015 from http://dailyindependentnig.com/2014/05/world-bank-report-poverty-nigeria/
- Emmanuel, F. T. 2008. The Poetics of Eco-activism in Ojaide's Tale of Harmattan. Ibadan Journal of English Studies. 4.5:172-182.Babatope Babalobi. 2008. Corruption

in Nigeria: causes and solutions. Retrieved 6 July, 2015 from http://assemblyonline.info/corruption-in-nigeria-causes-and-solutions/

- Harold Smith's Tribute Page. https://haroldsmithmemorial. wordpress.com/2011/01/05/legendary-harold-smith-speaks-about-nigeria/.
- "Poverty in Nigeria: Rich Country, Poor People" Research for social & economic development 2013. Retrieved 7 July 2015 from http://www.poverties.org/poverty-in-nigeria. html
- Thompson, E. F. (2008). Basic income and poverty alleviation in rural areas of west Africa. Ibadan: Evans Publishers Ltd.

CHAPTER THREE: HOPE: THE ONLY OPTION FOR THE MASSES?

- Nwagbara Kelechi 2015 "The Nigeria's Poliitical Drama" retrieved 14 July from www.naija.com/326142-nigerianpoliticans-and-nigerians.html
- Mustapha C. Shehu. 2015. "Memo to Nigerian Masses" Retrieved 14 July 2015 from www.gamji.com/article500/ MENS5812.htm

CHAPTER FOUR: IS LEADERSHIP THE MAIN PROBLEM OF NIGERIA?

- "Abraham Lincoln was One of the Worst Presidents". http:// www.debate.org/debates/Abraham-Lincoln-was-one-of-the-worst-presidents/1/ Achebe Chinua. 1983. The trouble with Nigeria. Fourth Dimension Publishing Co. Nigeria. Microsoft Encarta Dictionaries. 2009. Microsoft Corporation.

- Arrian of Nicomedia. "The Mutiny at Opis". http://www. livius.org/aj-al/alexander/alexander_t25.html
- Benjamin Constant, Political Writings, ed. and trans., Biancamaria Fontana (Cambridge: Cambridge University Press, 1988), 161-63.
- Chemers M. M. 2002. Cognitive, Social, and Emotional Intelligence of Transformational Leadership: efficacy and Effectiveness. In R. E. Riggio, S. E. Murphy, F. J. Pirozzolo (eds), Multiple Intelligence and leadership. Mahwah, New Jersey: Lawrence Erlbaum associates.
- Chinenye Leo Ochulor. 2011. "Failure of leadership in Nigeria" in American Journal of Social and Management Sciences. 2011; 265- 271.
- Ogbeidi M. Michael. 2012. "Political Leadership and Coruption in Nigeria since 1960: A Socio-e$conomic analysis" in Journal of Nigeria Studies. Volume 1 no 2. Fall 2012.
- "Otto von Bismarck". Encyclopaedia Britannica.
- "The Assassination of Julius Caesar, 44 BC." http://www. eyewitnesstohistory.com/caesar2.htm

CHAPTER FIVE: 55 YEARS AFTER: NIGERIA STILL IN SEARCH OF A LEADER

- Ademoyega Adewale. 2014. Why We Struck. Ibadan: Evans Brothers Limited.
- Daily Times (1966, January 16). The Editorial Column.
- Laing Aislinn. May 29, 2015. Nigeria's President Goodluck Jonathan hands over to former dictator Muhammadu Buhari. The Telegraph. Retrieved July 31, 2015, from www.telegrsph. co.uk/news/worldnews/africaandindianocean/11637544/

Nigerias-president-Goodluck-Jonathan-to-hand-over-to-former-dictator-Mohammadu-Buhari.html

- Odeh E. Lemuel. Analysis of Factors Inhibiting Democracy and Democratization in Nigeria, 1999-2007. The Fourth Republic in Nigeria: A Decade of Democratisation Reviewed. Eds T. N. Sunday & T. Wauam Eds. Aboki Publishers: Makurdi.
- Ogbeidi M. Michael. 2012. Political Leadership and Coruption in Nigeria since 1960: A Socio-economic analysis. Journal of Nigeria Studies. Volume 1 no 2. Fall 2012.
- Omodia S.M. 2012. Election, Governance and the Challenge of National Integration in the Nigerian Fourth Republic. British Journal of Arts and Social Sciences: British Journal Publishing, Inc. Vol.5 No.2: 2012

CHAPTER SIX: REMNANT LEADERS WITH TRUNCATED TENURES

- "Nigeria's past Military excuse for COUPS Since 1966 still thrives". http://eagleyereportconnect.blogspot.com.ng/2014/05/coup.html#sthash.mgIiKbUU.dpuf
- "Juxtaposing the late Murtala Muhammed legacies and the April polls" Vanguard, February 23, 2011.
- Siollun Max (2009, February 13). The Assassination of Murtala Muhammed. https://maxsiollun.wordpress.com/2009/02/13/the-assasination-of-murtala-muhammed/

CHAPTER SEVEN: REMNANT LEADERS WITH UNSUSTAINED LEGACIES

- Oduguwa Adedara S. (2012). Chief Obafemi Awolowo: The Political Moses. Trafford Publishing, United States.

CHAPTER EIGHT: CITIZENS AS DRIVERS OF NATIONAL DEVELOPMENT

- "About Nation Building". http://www.gemstoneng.org/about-nation-building.php
- "About Us". Saani Bello Foundation. http://www.sanibellofoundation.org/about.php
- Cable News Network (2015, April 29). "Flying doctor takes to the skies after sister's death". http://edition.cnn.com/2013/04/08/world/africa/ola-orekunrin-flying-doctors-nigeria/

CHAPTER NINE: IS DEMOCRACY A VIABLE OPTION FOR NIGERIA?

- Abidde, Sabella O. (2006, August 9). "Suggesting Military Democracy for Nigeria". http://www.nigeriansinamerica.com/suggesting-military-democracy-for-nigeria/
- Adeyinka, T.A and Ojo, E.O. Democracy in Nigeria: Practice, Problems and Prospects. Developing Country Studies. Vol 4, No 2, 2014

CHAPTER TEN: STRONG MEN OR STRONG INSTITUTIONS?

- Chirot, Daniel. 1979. Social Change in the Twentieth Century. Harcourt Brace Jovanovich Inc. New York, P. 2-3.
- Obama, Barack. 2009. Cited in Bolaji Akinyemi. 2012. "Leadership, Democracy and Development: A Paradigm Relationship, Inaugauration Lecture. Ondo State Government of Nigeria. Saturday, February , 23, P. 5.
- Gambari A. Ibrahim. 2008. 'The Challenges of Nations Building: The Case of Nigeria' at the First Year Anniversary Lecture of Mustapha Akanbi Foundation. 7, February.

CHAPTER ELEVEN: THE NECESSITY OF NATIONAL REORIENTATION ON VALUE SYSTEM

- Henslin, J. 2008. Sociology: a down-to-earth approach (9th ed.). Boston: Pearson International.
- Kluckhohn, C. 2005. Identifying societal values. Retrieved September 3 from www.orednet.org/jflory/20s/val_over_ ver2.
- NEEDS. 2004. National Economic Empowerment and Development Strategy 2004. Abuja: the NEEDS Secretariat, National Planning Commission.
- Osoba, S. 1996. Corruption in Nigerian historical perspectives. Review of African Political Economy. 69: 371-386.
- Teniola, E. 2015. Behold the Kuru Declaration. Vanguard News July 29, 3015. Retrieved from http://www.vanguardngr.com/2015/07/Behold-the-Kuru-declaration/ on September 3, 2015.

- Transparency International 2013. Corruption Perception Index 2013. Retrieved from http://www.transparency.org

CHAPTER TWELVE: GOOD NATIONAL VALUES PRODUCE GOOD NATIONAL LEADERS

- Ayokunnu Ojeniyi. 2006. Way out for Nigeria - The Value System way! Retrieved 31 August, 2015 from http://ojeniyiayokunnu.blogspot.com/2006/09/way-out-for-nigeria-value-system-way.html
- Ismaila Suleiman. 2009. Value re-orientation in the rebranding project in Nigeria: the role of education. A paper presented at the 27th annual conference of philosophy of education of Nigeria, 6th-9th October, 2009.
- Okechukwu D. Nnamani and Ogochukwu J. Iloh. 2014. Good Governance and National value: Where does Nigeria Stand at 53? International Journal of Democratic and Development Studies (IJDDS), Vol. 2, No 1, Jan., 2014

CHAPTER THIRTEEN: BUILDING STRONG NATIONAL SYSTEMS AND INSTITUTIONS FOR NIGERIA

- Achebe, Chinua. 1983. The Trouble with Nigeria. Enugu: Fourth Dimension Publishers.
- Dike, Victor. 2000. 'Leadership, Politics, and Social Change: Nigeria and the Struggle for Survival'. Africa Economic Analysis. Sacramenta California.
- Imobighe, Thomas. 2003. Nigerian Defence and National Security Linkages: A Framework of Analysis. Ibadan: Heinemann Books Plc.Nye,

- J. S. 1967.' Corruption and Political Development: A Cost-Benefit Analysis'. The American Political Science Review.

ABOUT PASTOR SUNDAY ADELAJA

Sunday Adelaja is the founder and senior pastor of the Embassy of God in Kiev Ukraine and the author of more than 300 books which are translated in several languages including Chinese, German, French, Arabic, etc.

A fatherless child from a 40 hut village in Nigeria, Sunday was recruited by communist Russia to ignite a revolution, instead he was saved just before leaving for the USSR where he secretly trained himself in the Bible while earning a Master's degree in journalism. By age thirty-three he had built the largest church in Europe.

Today, his church in Kiev has planted over a thousand daughter churches in over fifty countries of the world. Right now they plant four new churches every week. He is known to be the only person in the world pastoring a cross cultural church where 99% of his twenty five thousand members are white Caucasians.

His work has been widely reported by world media outlets like Washington Post, The wall street Journal, Forbes, New York times, Associated Press, Reuters, CNN, BBC, German, Dutch, French National television, etc.

Pastor Sunday had the opportunity to speak on a number of occasions in the United Nations. In 2007 he had the rare privilege of opening the United States Senate with prayers. He has spoken in the Israeli Knesset and the Japanese parliament along with several other countries. Pastor Sunday is known as an expert in national transformation through biblical principles and values.

Pastor Sunday is happily married to his "princess' Pastor Bose Adelaja. They are blessed with three children, Perez, Zoe and Pearl.

BOOKS BY PASTOR SUNDAY ADELAJA

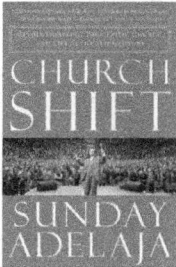

Churchshift: *Revolutionlize your faith, Church and life for the 21st Century.*

Money Won't Make you Rich: *God's Principles for True Wealth, Prosperity and Success.*

Time is Life: *History Makers Honor Time.*

Pastoring Without Tears: *It is possible to live and minister without sorrow and grief.*

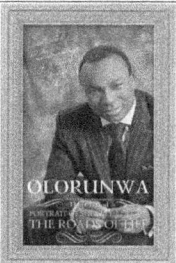

Olorunwa (There is God): *Portrait of Sunday Adelaja. THE ROADS OF LIFE.*

FOLLOW PASTOR SUNDAY ON SOCIAL MEDIA

Subscribe And Read Pastor Sunday's Blog:
WWW.SUNDAYADELAJABLOG.COM

Follow These Links And Listen To Over 200 Of Pastor
Sunday`S Messages Free Of Charge:
WWW.GODEMBASSY.COM/MEDIA

Follow Pastor Sunday On Twitter, 5 Words Of Wisdom Daily:
WWW.TWITTER.COM/SUNDAYADELAJA
…And Suggest Your Friends To Follow As Well!

Join Pastor Sunday's Facebook Page To Stay In Touch:

WWW.FACEBOOK.COM/PASTOR.SUNDAY.ADELAJA
…And Suggest Your Friends To Join As Well!

VISIT OUR WEBSITES FOR MORE INFORMATION
ABOUT PASTOR SUNDAY'S MINISTRY:
http://www.godembassy.com
http://www.pastorsunday.com
http://www.churchshift.org
http://www.sundayadelaja.de
http://www.sundayadelaja.com
http://www.adelaja.com

CONTACT

For distribution or to order bulk copies of this book, please contact us:

USA
CORNERSTONE PUBLISHING
info@thecornerstonepublishers.com
+1 (516) 547-4999 | www.thecornerstonepublishers.com

AFRICA
Sunday Adelaja Media Ltd.
Email: btawolana@hotmail.com
+2348187518530, +2348097721451, +2348034093699.

LONDON, UK
Pastor Abraham Great
abrahamagreat@gmail.com
+447711399828, +44-1908538141

KIEV, UKRAINE
pa@godembassy.org
Mobile: +380674401958

www.ingramcontent.com/pod-product-compliance
Lightning Source LLC
Chambersburg PA
CBHW021220090426
42740CB00006B/296